INTERNET LOVE: HOW I MET MY WIFE

A TRAVEL DOCUMENTARY

BY DENNIS CLEASBY

Published in the United States by Cathedral Art Gallery Records
P.O. Box 808, Glenwood Landing, NY, USA 11547-0808

Text and Photography ©, 2008 DENNIS CLEASBY

The moral and ethical right of the author has been asserted.

Endless gratitude goes to my sister Constance for her editing help.

You are invited to also purchase a larger version of this book in its
First Edition (ISBN 978-0-9817015-0-9) in an 8.5 X 11 size, with 188
pages of full color artworks and photography by the author.
Contact: www.denniscleasby.com
This book has been composed in iWorks/ Pages, and Adobe Acrobat
Pro. Photography is created with an Olympus E-300/ E Volt Camera.

Library of Congress Number 2008903142

SECOND EDITION

ISBN-13: 978-0-9817015-1-6
ISBN-10: 0-9817015-1-5

Printed in the United States

ISBN: 978-0-9817015-1-6

9 780981 701516

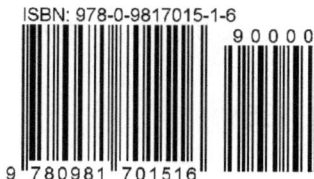

*FOR DIANA
WHO HAS OPENED MANY
DOORS TO HAPPINESS.*

Forward by Diana Cleasby

In this book Dennis wants to share with the world a small part of his life with me (A foreigner from Colombia) and tell about his commitment to our marriage. We never thought we would find true love until we found each other through the Internet. Since our marriage we have easy and difficult times, but day-to-day the relationship grows and we build our story. We are common and simple people who separate the obstacles between two different countries, cultures, customs, and languages. In modern times real love exists. Ours is one of those stories. I invite you to read this book. (Translation by Dennis)

Chapters Index

Chapter 1. The Beginnings

The sound of a woman's voice is like that of a songbird. That song is my wife's voice. She is a bird that is of an unknown species or genome. She resonates the song of a bird that is heard for the first time ever. I listen to her with the awe and wonder of a child discovering life. Diana is my wife from Colombia. We did not hear each other's voice for months because we communicated by email. Despite this, her "tone of voice" came through in her writing. I had an inclination toward foreigners. I had a premonition. My day with destiny was designed for the specific type of person I was looking for. The computer was my compass and tool. A series of bad dates, small successes, trial and error, and good luck lead me to meet my wife. In the short time since our wedding we have traveled to many countries in the Americas, Ireland, and found deep love that grows daily. The photographs on this book were taken by me along our journey. While we travel I do watercolors as well. There have been critics and skeptics that foolishly doomed our fate. We had insurmountable odds against us, and the challenge is still alive. This is our love story.

Perhaps the biggest reason I am writing this book is to record our life together and process what we are both living through; the good and the bad. Self expression ignites healing and creates a sense of balance in the midst of life's ups and downs. Creative soul searching permits the adult to relax and be a child again. This is not a manual for finding a wife, but one needle in the haystack of romantic stories. Our story is universal to the challenges that face any relationship and what happens once love's initial dust settles. When I was young I was very drawn to realistic art. I prefer to paint and photograph realistic views. I also prefer "reality literature" and writers who comment on life as they see it and live it. I have been able to work though our marriage and sharpen my awareness of the struggles that appear when marrying a woman twenty years younger than myself, from a different culture, from a place that is less complicated, and in many ways more pure, like my wife.

I was looking. I was actively seeking the right person. And I knew it was not going to be easy. I wasn't looking for a quick shallow fix to my situation. I was looking for the correct characteristics in a person where growth in a committed relationship was the biggest potential. Three years earlier I had come out of a long term, bad relationship where the mix was tumultuous. I wasn't that dead set on marriage. I failed at that thirty years before. I knew I didn't want anyone like I had lived with before, and I knew I'd travel to the far reaches of the globe to find her. After six months of the Internet and phone calls I went to Colombia to see who this woman really was.

I keep a journal. Sections of this book (the second half) will be my travel journal writings, while the first section is a more direct biography addressing my new marriage and the life that lead me to a state of commitment. I will also include journals from our travels. I often write in my journal while I float with the wind in my kayak near my house on Long Island. I've kept a journal since I was 14 and traveled to Pakistan with my family in 1965. That's when I began writing. Back then I wanted to keep some kind of record of what I would see while traveling and I have been disciplined enough every since (forty-three years) to keep up the ritual. Now my writing has two different modes of expression between writing on a computer, not a wise thing to do in a kayak, and writing by hand my inner thoughts while I meditate on the water with my journal. When I was going through a tremendous emotional change, due to the end of a relationship, I bought a kayak. Soon I found myself writing in my journal while floating on the water. The two seemed to lend themselves to me finding inner peace. I don't kayak for exercise.

Here is a recent journal entry since my marriage:

When I come back here, on the water, the feeling is different in the sense that I'm not lonely; in the past much of my time was spent in a state of suffering from loneliness. It's amazing what living with another person does for that. I also realize a kind of enjoyment that comes from the quest to not be lonely, the searching. Now, during my day, I seem to remind myself from time to time just what it was like to be so alone. I also enjoy the small disturbances that come when interrupted and asked to attend to some daily event. I see it from two sides. I love the companionship and loved the pain in the past; or rather, I had become addicted to the painful aspect of loneliness. I certainly know all the companionship doesn't come without a price. The companionship doesn't leave as much time to be creative, or to go out alone in my kayak.

There is also the added dimension of being closely involved. Diana lost her grand mothers pearl earring last night (We had gone to Thanks Giving dinner at my cousins in Manhattan.) When we got home I heard her voice from the other room. The emotion was piercing. "My original pearls are missing. My grandmother's original pearls are gone." It was one pearl earring. "Original" was an added word that her English usage made the event seem even more drastic. I felt the woman I love suffer therefore I was suffering. It's a huge vulnerability to be exposed to another's raw feelings, especially if one is so intimately close. It's not like hearing about another's problems with their love life. It's a deep, deep emotion knowing how important this pearl was to my wife. In the morning we went out to the car and retraced our path looking for the missing pearl. We looked, she returned to the house, but I kept looking. Sure enough I was overjoyed to locate the single pearl under the passenger seat. Now, in all honesty a pearl to me might as well be a simple stone. I could care less about jewelry, but the pain in her voice was horrible to feel.

I'm thinking, "What if we have a child". A mother's anguish and the added emotion of a small, innocent child's love is a scary thing to me. Diana wants a child. I want to wait. I don't care if her biological clock runs out in six years. I want to be in a position to be financially and emotionally secure. I want the relationship to be as solid as it can be. The relationship is still new. It needs to be more concrete through friendship and acquaintance. Diana is a natural mother. She goes wild at the sight of any baby; while shopping, watching TV, or in the car. She's there, like a trigger going off the second a tiny creature appears. She also tries the convincing, opposite, extreme with me. "Ok, so you don't like babies". Thirty-five years of solo artistic pursuit isn't easily replaced by the sudden urge to make a small me (Dennis). I'd like to father Christ, or the messiah. I'm a little serious, and also fooling. If I'm going to be a father the child needs to be a great benefit to all humanity. This is only reflective of the pressure I put on myself to be "great" and productive. Also to be a positive role model and teacher. At best I'd be a good provider. It's not enough to be a financial provider, like my father, but also an emotional provider, vastly different from my father.

So goes the kind of subject matter I write in an informal way; bouncing around, spilling my life like wine and cleaning up while out in the kayak. If I didn't do this I might be alcoholic like my mother was in her later years.

In my life I have had five major geographic changes: Panama, California, Pakistan, Nebraska, and New York. With New York being the last move twenty-two years ago. I know what it is like to be up-rooted and thrown into a new environment. I have some knowledge of what my new wife may be going through as a new arrival from Colombia. Unlike Diana, most of my changes came at an early age. Not when I was professionally and emotionally rooted culturally, and living at home with my parents while practicing Catholicism. She is the proverbial bird that has flown the golden cage, but the bird needs shelter, familiarity, and nourishment.

I was born in Omaha Nebraska. My mother was a devote Catholic. My father was a non-devote Episcopalian who converted for the marriage. My parents had five children. We grew up in California and my mother always wanted to return to Nebraska. It was a constant theme of discontentment with the Southern California pace and longing for real winters, and four seasons that returned most of the family to the Mid-west in 1967. This move came after my father completed a two year job assignment in Pakistan.

My parent's marriage was horrible, especially in my teenage years. Infidelity was a secret my father hide from the children, but unfortunately not my mother. Divisions over religion, how to raise the children, and money issues would eventually split the family into two parental camps; mom's side and dad's side. Nobody benefited from the violent upheavals, strict disciplinary measures, and lack of close parental supervision, but there were early years of nurturing, comfort, and closeness. Our family evolved out of the post war 1950's view of reality; church going peppered with bigotry, strong patriotism, materialism, and a sense that family was an impenetrable force. I remember peaceful Sunday mornings and pancake breakfasts in the park, as well as dishes being broken into a thousands pieces on Christmas morning as my parents argued.

The last time our entire family unit was together was in Lahore, Pakistan in 1965. My father took a job overseas which sent the whole family (five siblings and my parents) through several countries. We all arrived at our new home only to be uprooted shortly thereafter. A war between India and Pakistan sent the children with my mother to Tehran, Iran. What seemed like an inconvenient and a dangerous time turned out to be the last time we were all together. My older brother and sister returned to the States. I spent three months in Tehran and eventually returned to Lahore with my mother and two younger sisters. Before our evacuation to Tehran, my mother would lead the family in prayer each and every night by candlelight. The Lahore City black out locked us all into a hotel room where we would say the rosary, pray for peace, and complain about having to be on our knees without any soft church pews to cushion the pain. I was fifteen years old.

During this war one memorable event was my father's near arrest as a spy. (My father had a minor in photography from the University of Southern California, his major was architecture.) He and I went on a walk to take photographs. Not a good idea during a war. "The two foreign spies" were flushed out of their hotel room only to be briefly interrogated by military police and thus given a stern warning to keep the camera in the hotel room. My father was an arrogant American who wasn't about to be intimidated by a bunch of "Paks". After all he was white, superior in intellect, and a towering six feet four inches tall. He would intimidate adults who challenged him and equally intimidate his children and wife. In fairness he was a product of his time; a generation bent from war, and drunk with over confidence from victory. No one was as correct as he. Elvis was not welcome in our house. Perry Como and Andy Williams had a reverent place.

The undefined end of our family began in Pakistan and continued into the next few years. When we returned to the United States my oldest sister moved back to California, the rest of us to Nebraska. I began to experiment with drugs (mostly marijuana) and turned to music and art, like so many others of my generation. The family was in a state of deterioration; my mother began to drink, my father had an affair with his secretary. The final tragic chapter of our family came and went without being realized at the time. My older sister was shot (murdered) by her boyfriend who was a cop. He was never prosecuted, in fact the whole event was conveniently announced to be an accidental death. There were no witnesses. The truth has been buried along with so many other family secrets. It took me years to regain respect for law enforcement and the judicial system. A few years ago I spent months trying to reopen my sisters case, but an "accidental death" isn't considered a homicide, and not worth the time of the Huntington Beach Police Chief. My parents were nowhere near capable of insisting on a trial while their personal lives were in such shambles. My involvement in the antiwar movement dovetailed its way into increased counter-culture activities, further from my real family and closer to my family of musician-friends.

How do two people from two separate worlds dance into a loving embrace? Hope and imagination are the source of much love on the planet. In this age of emails and phones finding love is just as far away as a fingers touch on a keypad. For some reason I had this idea that my significant other had to come through the Internet. I had been "Internet dating" through a Costa Rican web site and joined one of the big national online services, but that seemed to be a dead end. My training in a Masters program at

Long Island University gave me some inclination about the "future" and how people were meeting, but I never entered a chat room (even to this day), and I cautiously signed up for two or three dating services. I had this hunch that my destiny was going to be unconventional, after a very emotionally draining break up three years earlier.

How does a single man meet a woman in this day and age without first giving a negative impression? I was divorced, in my mid-fifties, and had a slight spare tire around my gut. I also see myself as so unconventional that I'm not mainstream female material. Yes, I hold a job, and have a reasonable salary for an educator, but years of poverty and a dire dedication to my art and music have lead me to be eccentric and a little, if not a lot, anti-establishment.

To attract a younger woman was a fantasy and a little strange considering the last woman I had been with for eight years was eleven years older than I. Diana is twenty years younger than me. I wrote her two or three emails with a friend from my job, Flor, giving me an introduction first. Diana never answered. I admit I was fishing and dropping more than one line in more than one lake. I had emails from Costa Rica, did occasional speed dating (which was a fun social outing for me), and swayed between feeling like a total loser to a prime catch. My emotional make up is a ferris wheel of over confidence, on top, to a dejected hermit hiding every flaw from the world, on the bottom. I called Flor a few times asking what happened. She never heard back.

Flor is Colombian; her sister, Margarita, was Diana's classmate in a speech pathology program at the University. Margarita told Diana, through Flor, that she had a husband for her. Diana ignored everybody and mostly me. I stupidly sent Diana a photograph of me. She thought that I was too old for her. The balding head and long curly hair were even more foreign.

Somewhere in my Internet juggling and many phone calls to Flor, I got an email from Diana that was three lines long. She took the bait. She loves to tell how I was interested, and how she knew, in Colombian culture, that a woman never answers a stranger's email unless she is loose or looking for money. "It is not the custom in my country to answer a man's emails". I don't know who caught whom, but little by little our words formed into a union. Things didn't start out with a bang, more like a small trickle of occasional hellos. Behind the small wall of words I was sensing character and consistency. I knew as long as a friendship was pursued I couldn't be hurt, I couldn't be rejected, and the distance meant it was all safe fun.

My impression of Diana's first photograph was equally negative by the way. She looked over-sized, over aged, had a big bottle of Coke in front of her, held a giant purse, and was sitting hugging her nephew. How unromantic! What possible damage could come from an innocent email now and then? Sometimes we are all looking for glitz when the subtle background is true reality. If you aren't aware of the falseness of your own delusions, delusion will get the better of you. So I kept writing, more in love with my grand ideals of love. At the same time I was paying attention to that quiet voice within that always makes fun of me, myself, and I. If things are too serious it can alienate another person. No one wants someone who is desperate, but I was getting pretty tired of looking for a mate and even more so of being lonely. I know how to keep busy, but no one knows how to avoid that gnawing absence of a partner gone after they have lived with someone, only to become single again.

The "next person" is replacing a whole series of vacancies and expectations from the past. We all shadow dance with our previous experiences and if we are lucky enough we learn a new step and let go of the past just enough to see the new beginning. We pass over a threshold and a slight change of light causes us to ask ourselves, did I just encounter a glimmer of the future, or is this the "same old same old". Is my imagination getting the best of me again? Did my entire life just change, or is that me flying a kite like a child wondering where the wind carries such wondrous gifts. That tiny line of string stretches high and we know at the end of it all someone else is dangling a thread from heaven, tugging just enough to keep us in awe and not enough to drag us away. Both hearts are grounded in hope and fortunate to reverse the roles; being held firmly at one point in time, and reeled back to earth by patience and a need to feel homeward bound, and to belong.

In February 2005 I was in Costa Rica. I had a hernia surgery and was recouping, riding my bicycle (against my doctor's orders) to the Internet café, longing for Diana's words. As seldom as the early emails had been the now widening interest kept growing. All we were really doing was being friends, and telling each other our daily lives, and our life stories. At some point on that trip I realized that I was very interested in Diana. We began writing in November of 2006. By February I was at the Internet café like clockwork. I didn't think I had anything "in the bag" and certainly wasn't in love, but I was very intrigued. I remember talking about her as my cousin Frank and I were building some shelves in the sweltering Costa Rican heat. I said something like; "She seems to be the person who is standing out the most right now". I was calling her every few days. Frank was listening to me compare her to this woman or that, but I was going beyond intrigue. I would ride my bicycle to the Internet café and write, maybe even call in the same day.

Frank was a wonderful sounding board. Being cousins we have known each other since some of my earliest childhood memories; sliding down a hill in boxes through the leaves. This was a family visit to Omaha in the 1950's. We were living in California. Frank and his brother, John, put me in the cardboard box and I'd fly down the hill. Years later I saw the very spot and the memory returned. The hill was a tiny embankment. Actually, there was no hill at all. My memory is always bigger than reality, or a child learns to exaggerate.

The beginnings of my relationship with Diana were slow and situations were well paced in time. My family history, my divorces, the distance between us, and not wanting to get burned, all concluded in a "wait and see" attitude. Diana had been engaged twice, both times ended in heartbreak for her. The safest way to begin for both of us was a seemingly impersonal medium; emails. The quality of a person can't be seen immediately in emails. All

16

relationships can truly only develop with the passage of time no matter how lonely and willing the candidates. If you are filling a void in your personal life or looking for that one substantial significant other, nothing happens over night. Over night success is a myth. One-night disasters are even more common. Beyond all the surface needs and desires, if there is a good self image and desired goal of a healthy relationship, it will happen for those who give an honest attempt.

Maybe we had luck. Maybe we had divine providence. Maybe we had lived through enough failures to be ready for success. I can't give a clear reason why we clicked and continue to relate constructively. The odds against us were tremendous. Right now we are approaching that two-year mark, but I feel confident we have been through the worst. We've met other couples that say how tough the first year is. I know we won't quit or give up on each other. I have put forth an extra effort to make her life here as comfortable as possible. I'm not the kind of man sitting around waiting to be served or taken care of. I spent so many years alone any added dimension to the day-to-day life is greatly appreciated. Diana says she would never write a book about her personal life. I've been writing for years, but never went public with such private information. That can be a problem. To share has no guarantees.

Diana and I have been left by others and rejected. Maybe subconsciously we found in each other a trusting partner we feel safe with. Our qualities attracted each other but nothing was sudden. I've lived long enough to know what is correct and good, verses what is impulsive and destructive. The beginning and end of a story is what's important. This is our beginning out in the open. This is a reality story. The technology that exists in the world makes for better communication but the personal qualities of the users is key to taking life to the next level. Technology is a new tool for lovers. Love will never be better or worse because of it. Love is eternal beyond the toys of humans.

Chapter 2. Internet Dating

Dating without seeing a person, or hearing their voice is a little scary. Today, with visual messaging this is different. We did not use the live camera links. If Flor had not told me about Diana before, the apprehensions I had may have dwindled into total apathy. Little by little I was losing interest in other woman online, or had met in person, and I was finding Diana to be emotionally sound, intelligent, and punctual. There is no error in realizing that the process of dating is based on high expectations, sometimes too high. Illusion is also at play, more so on the Internet. Common downfalls of relationships occur when all expectations are not based in real mutual experiences. New technologies offer us more opportunities and choices, but the rest is up to how we are as people. Technology does not make us more ethical. Communication technologies bring us closer together, but that doesn't change the qualities of our personalities. Who we are, and our need to be loved, will never change.

I have kept all our emails. I had other email "dates", some for months and some lasting only a few volleys. Honestly what inspired me to bring our relationship to reality was an exhausting pace of writing that went on night after night. I was filling my loneliness with hours of emails. Yes, there was distraction at play, but there was something else taking form. It is not often I am with a loss of words. Short emails were not the kind of exchange that was taking place. We talked about our day-to-day lives in detail. I knew when she was getting home and off work. She worked two jobs, so her time was precious and that time was being shared with me. I knew about her family and friends. I wasn't deceiving her about my activities because there was nothing to hide. The same was true of Diana.

The strange dimension to all the Internet communication was that neither of us spoke each other's language. I bought a translation program a year before. That somewhat did the job, but it was down right weird language at times. She told me once she had acne on her back. The translation program turned this intimate

18

information into reading she had sprouts growing on her back. Many of the words made reading the emails a guessing process. Much of the reading was an in depth search for, "What the hell is she saying?". I attribute my patience in all this puzzle reading to my creative side. If I was able to write music in metaphors I surely was able to read messages that could be pieced together to make some sense. When I look back there was as much laughter at the weird language as serious time invested in a growing bond. Today Diana tells me she fell in love with me through my words. Her words were jumbled and incorrect because of the translation program, but sweet as honey. I focused on her personality behind the words, other wise I would have missed her completely. If a woman is willing to write every day and the man is also writing, what's to stop things from going to the next level of friendship?

I am a real freak for punctuality. Being early is a must; that makes being on time easy. Sometimes I'd get home and an email would be waiting for me. Diana had written in the morning before she went to work. The basis of our discussion was simple and easy, while the technology kept weaving us closer and closer. The effort to keep the communication going was glue for our friendship. I wasn't letting my expectations run ahead of me. After all, there were thousands of miles and many differences between us. Yet the feelings were growing. The relationship that dominated my life was with Diana even though we were thousands of miles apart. Marriage wasn't my goal. I was happy to be in the relationship, but also asking myself why I wasn't being more practical and looking close to home. I came to a point where I was either going to let go, terminate, or find a way to bring Diana here. The only way to bring her here was to marry her. Yes, we could have made many visits back and forth but we didn't. At some junction in our Internet dating I had to make a decision as to what I really wanted. I did not want to lose what had become so real and important. I knew a Catholic woman would never opt for living together. It came down to all or nothing. The "all" had more obstacles than nothing.

This is an email around the same times as Saint Valentine's Day. Some misunderstanding was in the emails. Diana had told me her needs in a relationship and thought she might have been too blunt. I was happy to see her mature expectations and was not the least bit concerned that she was being so up front. She had visited a dermatologist and was upset about her acne. I compensated my word choice in a way that would make the translation work better. I sent the following email.

Hello Diana,

I did receive your email yesterday. I was very tired. I have no problems with the skin doctor.

I do not understand when you think you offended me. How is this? I never felt offended. What are you referring to? I am not of the temperament to be offended. I am only offended by falsehood. This is not a part of you. You have only stated what you feel. This is honest. Your conditions for love are nothing to feel angry about. I respect your vision of what is necessary for love. This is a healthy need for love to grow and become real.

The computer translations are very unclear. The words are much jumbled. I do not understand all you say because I do not read Spanish. Many times the computer does not correctly give a word in English. This is my only frustration. You are not the source of this. It is the computer that will not give me a clear meaning. I want to learn more Spanish so I can understand your words better.

Today I went for the test. Everything is fine and well. The doctor has given me the approval for the surgery.

Tonight I went to dinner at a neighbor's house. She works at my school. She is the head of the music department. She has a Jacuzzi in her house. This was very relaxing.

Tomorrow there is a big snowstorm coming. There will be very deep snow. I will be home and enjoy this day while I watch the snow.

I will call you on Sunday. I will treat myself well on Valentines Day and I will think of you and wish you were here with me. Thank you for the moment of engaging my secret passion.
Love and Kisses, Dennis

INTERNET LOVE: HOW I MET MY WIFE

This is an email from Diana a few days before Valentines Day. I haven't changed the translation from the computer program. It shows some of the obvious difficulties in reading and trying to understand her words. Words that are misspelled or not recognizable are not processed in the program. These words come out as they were originally put into the computer. I apologize to my readers on how difficult the following emails may be to read. This is a word for word example of what I was reading.

As so you did not receive my card I sent to you 3 cards so that at least 1 was coming to you solita, anyhow although it is late happily it gives of San Valentin, I am glad that at least you could have spoken with your Superiors and that you were exhibiting what you were thinking: .... With this message he sent to you 2 photos in the first one (family Keeps silent about Diaz) there are my brother, his wife and his 2 kids, my nephews, name of girl is Laura has 4años, the child you already knew it his name is Sebastian and is the light of me eyes, I adore it he is a noble polite tender child it is really a great personita the muñequita has always been too attached to his breast I also want her very much but the child is a more attached alos of my house. .... In the second photo they are my breast and this is my dad so that you know them and you know who we are we,
I hope that you should have received the mail, who sends to you in the hours dela that you it have read and understood especially the understood one if not and s this way he would suggest you to say it again say to you that many things that you should want that you were understanding immediately DIANA sent to you another message.

In this mail he sent to you the photo of my dad and of my breast, in other he had said to you that that hiba the photo of them but I do not stay here in another mail there was the photo of all my famila, my dad, my breast, my brother my 2 nephews, my brother and I,..

In 2 photo of this mail we appear my brother Francisco and I in the moment have the cabelllo tinturado and tinture a bit the eyebrows see me the eyes small, but there is we are really as we are, in the actuality, he remembers that my hair really is dark but I felt like the painting doing to me and I am already as bored the root in the cabelllo sees me super dark and the clear cabelllo, in end until again me of for putting the hair of the color that has always been,

Still I am thinking that I happen with your cards he had written to you a few so pretty messages was saying to you so many things, that sorrow that they should not come to you,...

One has not forgotten me that tomorrow is your surgery at 6:00 a.m. I it have super earring and have asked GOD that the surgery should be the whole success that you are calm that you are very well that you do not sit pains he remembers that I am accompanying you spiritually and with the prayer I hope that really you should receive these messages remembers tomorrow I am called you thousand kisses think you and love you very much.
Diana Marcela

No, she did not send me a photograph of her breasts! This is a translation fluke that had me laughing. The reference is to "mother", but for some strange reason the translation comes out breast. Maybe I was secretly wishing for the other photograph, but this was her family we were discussing. These are proper people. I knew it. I could puzzle words into context, but it was very distracting. Many times I asked for a better explanation of her emails. I asked her to make the sentences short, but later learned that in Spanish sentences are long and a comma is used more often than a period. I really thought her grammar was terrible. Still I knew she was highly educated. The following is a short email I sent before my visit to her country. I had gone to a friend's birthday party and was late in writing her. I used the shortest possible sentences and kept my topics clear.
Hello Again,

I am home from the restaurant. This was special for Victoria. There were seven of us. The crowd at our table was very noisy. We were the last table to leave the restaurant before closing.

Dear One I do not care if you are chubby. This is only a veil of your personality. I care about love and what we create

22

together. I am sure we will both feel shy when we meet. My expectations are realistic. We have a safe friendship and we both have an equal investment and risk, so we will both enter into the unknown together. I think the difficult part will be when we have to leave each other. We are in a new place that is unique to both of us. We will make the best of life.

I go to sleep now. Yes, I will dream about. I send you peace as you sleep.
Love, Dennis

This email was before my visit to Diana's country. The puzzle of putting together what was exactly being said had the additional benefit of my limited Spanish, and by this time the phone calls that had began were crucial to our exchanges. The phone calls were an opportunity to clear up what was actually being written.

HELLO.; you aclaro PAPASITO Y DADDY IS FOR MAN; FOR THE WOMAN IT IS MAMASITA; OR MAMATA; THAT IS TO SAY; MAN OR WOMAN ADJOINS, or nice, that one a nice way of calling someone who appreciates of my papaeles pair rich coast I tell you, today they asked me for a new role, the role of the das. is demoradito, I have to get in ahead of the next sdabado wings 4 of tomorrow to manage to be attended in the week it is impossible for that I have, that to be wings 7:30 of the morning in the work and they did not give me permission of being absent in the week.

As soon as wing electronic direction that you ask me I tell you that I have not opened it, I saw a program on the park of the coffee and there this direction was appearing, if you cannot find search in the Internet, tourist Park of the coffee (Armenia - COLOMBIA) and there you will find information, I would love that you were reading something of the tourism in COLOMBIA, for when you avenge, do not come so lost, M and he would love knowing something about your GODS, of course, if you quda easy, and you are not very tired, Yesterday do not manage to write to you in the night because I came much late and very tired, anyhow, I will try it, not and asguro not at all, I am going pair the clinic to visit my dad, then, must be with uma compañera.hoy I had some accidents, s caundo go so far as to work, in the grill ompi the bluyin, I went away to, l work of washed face, by which it was taken of the tared, today I belonged to jean, camisetica, and tennnis, there got lost me the buckle of the tail of horse that I do to myself normally, then what today teeny-weeny camisetica was never of covered jean, tennis, without makeup and of free hair, today I it was an entire disorder, and me the flowers rained that according to my partners of trabsajo and according to the boys estanba with the excited beauty, I go. normally areglada to the work, with little makeup but pintadita, with the taken or brushed hair, never so disorganized as today, and com I say to you the first time that I receive so many praises and pirom pos really that this world is crazy,

You write to ME in tucarta that sews them s between us they are fine and I, I think the same thing, little by little we know each other, be that in the future we have an affectionate, serious relation or we do not know each other and little by little there are happening the things of my part fodder, you are a super important person and I hope to have you a lot of time as my friend and if the things go further away., better, I would not become brave, I swear it to you that not. you look like to me a brilliant person, and I am happy to meet you in letters and hope to be able to meet you personally, love you very much very much very much, I Love the detalle that you had with VICTORIA that he says very good things of you, I hope that you should have had a pretty day::::: DIANA MARCELA

The coffee park is a tourist attraction or resort we were talking about visiting. The tail of horse is a ponytail. Some of the message is obviously esoteric, but the endless translation within the translation was a real endeavor. I tried to write short sentences and pick words that had a common Latin base. She said some of my writing was confusing but on my side it was a real effort.

This following email was sent after we became engaged. It was in late May when we were preparing for filing the immigration papers. A planned visit by Diana to Costa Rica never materialized because the bureaucratic red tape between the two countries is very slow. But we were able to use some of the same documentation she had already begun to gather.

Hello Light, I have completed all most every part of the seven forms. I have only a few empty lines. The book I bought has been very helpful. I will look into the best place to have the medical examination. This needs to take place after the wedding. I prepared as much of the data on you I could. The part about your employment history for the last five years is empty. I feel confident this is going to be easy. I know I was worried last week, but my worries motivated me to look into this situation. We will complete the final documents together and check each others work. We will be an excellent team.

Please bring all the documents you prepared to visit Costa Rica. They may be useful. The police records, the proof of financial status, and proof of employment may all be needed.

I have been trying to plan our finances for the summer. I get paid on June 24 for two months, but do not receive another pay check until September. So I have to set aside three months rent, the phone bill, and money for food. I am planning for the wedding ring, the marriage, and money for our travels. I also need to take money to Costa Rica to pay the lawyer and the electricity for a year. I have automatic payment for the electricity from my bank account. All looks good. We will have enough money to get through the summer. I have a good job thank God.

Tomorrow I will go fishing again. Two men from my job are going. We will use the boat of one of the men. This time we will not use the kayak. The weather is going to be good. I don't work on Monday because it is a holiday. So I get three days to relax, clean the house, and finish all my loose ends.

Ok I will call you at 8:30. I think I said 9:30 this morning. I'll call later if you are not home at 8:30.

I love you. I miss you. I need to talk too. It is not the same as emails. I need to hear your voice. It is still light outside so I will go for a walk and send you kisses in the air.
I love you, Dennis

Diana has said she fell in love with me through my writing. Yet I'm sure the spirit of my personality was much more apparent than my writings with a translation program. Being around foreigners and my early years of living in Spanish speaking cultures made me adapt to languages. As I look back I see how difficult building a bridge between us was. We are still building this bridge every day. Each builder needs a willing and extremely open heart, first and foremost. The happiness we now share made it well worth our efforts. Honestly, it took tremendous effort!

Chapter 3. The Wedding

We were married on July 6, 2006. On July first Diana flew from Colombia through Miami. I was able to fly her here on a voucher from American Airlines that had bounced me from a flight in Costa Rica a few months earlier. Diana called me from Miami but I had already left for the airport. When I got to the airport the flight screen said her flight was delayed and arriving at a specific gate. The parking garage at the airport was closed and I had to take shuttle bus to the terminal. I arrived two and a half hours early to make sure I'd be on time. I promised her on the phone, after many prompts, that I would be waiting for her.

Despite all my planning I was late. I went back by shuttle to the car to eat a banana and some food figuring I had plenty of time. The shuttle was late. I got to the terminal and the gate had been changed to another building. I ran as fast as I could. Diana was with a woman she had met on the airplane. She was Colombian too. They had been discussing alternatives; the woman offered Diana a place to stay for the night. I was twenty minutes late and Diana knew no one else's phone number in New York. She was in a state of turmoil and fright. I was out of breath.

Our airport embrace was real and nothing like the awkward first meeting in the airport in Colombia. (In Medellin we shook hands.) We soon had the bags in the car, after a long shuttle ride, and we were off to the apartment. In the car I gave my future bride a real kiss, not the kind where one feels they are being watched.

The next day we made arrangements for her to get her hair and makeup done by a friend of Flor's (Our "love connection" and the maid of honor). We went to visit Flor with her husband, Orlando, and her child, Alijandro. Diana had never met Flor even though they had talked on the phone. We had lunch and talked about the wedding plans. There was another woman there also. This friend of Flor's was also a speech therapist and had come to the States through a marriage. The marriage broke up and the woman told her war story to Diana. In the conversation the topic of the wedding dress came up. On a second visit a couple of days later the women took a look at Diana's dress. It was not approved! The woman said it was way to informal and not acceptable.

I got wind of this in the car afterwards. Diana was very upset. I was livid. Between my anger at this total stranger who thought it her right to be a judge, and trying to keep a good impression of my character to my wife to be, I was steaming inside. What is wrong with people? I had a bad impression of this woman and it was worse now. Even though the entire afternoon passed in the Spanish language I was very aware of the subtle game at play. I never saw the dress until the wedding day when Diana walked around the corner of the house with Flor's brother as her escort. But the next day I took Diana to several department stores to look at dresses. It took me hours but I finally convinced Diana the dress she and her mother had spent weeks looking for was good enough. And indeed it was.

The second day we spent just being together. I took Diana for a ride in the car where we saw the local scenery, the bays, the beaches, and President Theodore Roosevelt's home in Oyster Bay. After we had a home cooked meal in the backyard of the house. I was more interested in getting to know her than sitting in social environments with others. My instincts were to put her at ease and take some of the extra pressure off her. She was doing fine considering all the new excitement.

That night we began to organize the papers for our visit to the marriage licensing office in Oyster Bay. I had gone there the week before and made sure that Diana brought all the correct papers, and made sure there would be no glitches in our plans. I had spent months preparing for this wedding. Online I bought a book from the government, "Marriage Through the Green Card". Every "T" had to be crossed, and every letter and line perfect. I sent Diana a list of requests, via the emails, on what exactly had to be brought. I spent an hour copying and scanning documents for the wedding certificate. There was something missing and terribly wrong. A document with a seal was outdated.

I will preface the next few paragraphs with a warning to my readers. Sometimes I am an ass, and not the four legged type. My anger is a wild animal that needs to be harnessed and additionally caged. I have no excuse for my bad behavior other than a screwed up and a violent childhood. I know better but my body chemistry has a vile habit of exploding from time to time. Did I say I can be an ass? I am embarrassed by my outburst and fully aware that I didn't deserve to be given a second chance. Diana was suffering enough and I made her night a living hell. She was in a state of panic, crying her eyes out and had flown to a foreign country to be with a maniac. That night I told her to get out of the house. Now everyone knows what a jerk I am. One document had a slight error, enough to stop the wedding.

I did retract my words but they were very damaging. Thank God she didn't listen to me and we managed to calm down and get through the discussion the next morning. I still hear about my unfortunate use of vocabulary and weaknesses from time to time. My own stupidity still troubles me. I was fighting with a shadow that didn't exist in this dear woman. I was acting like everything I hated about my father and how he treated my mother. I occasionally carry an explosive demon that rears its' ugly head out of my psyche. The pressure to get it right was passed. I was mad, but more specifically I was afraid of failure. A clerical glitch and the arrogant perfectionist inside of me doomed the marriage. What was wrong with me?

The next morning I was relieved Diana was still there but scared as hell at the same time. The county offices opened at nine in the morning. We arrived at nine fifteen. The elderly woman I had asked many questions of, the week before, was out for the day. This seemed to be a bad omen. Another woman was at the next desk and had remembered me. We proceeded with every expectation of being denied the marriage certificate but sat politely. A cool casual mood didn't hurt, under my skin I was screaming like the night before. The birth certificate had an error! The woman only said, "Oh, they made a mistake on the date". True, but she saw everything else was in order. Diana jabbed me on the side as the woman turned away to type information. I was frozen and the polite demeanor of my smile was twice as frozen. I didn't dare look at Diana.

The papers weren't completely correct, any in-depth search of the documents would prove repeated correct dates, but nothing was being hidden. The birthday was the same as on the passport, it was ten years off. It truly was a typing error, as the woman had noted, but in my ragging quest for exact compliance I was convinced that it all had to be without ANY mistakes. The certificate was issued and our day took on an air of light-headed relaxation. I swear had the other clerk been working my fiancé would have been riding an airplane back to Colombia to get the darn birth certificate corrected so we could be married. That would have taken about three months considering the bureaucracy and insane difficulties Diana had already gone through getting everything notarized and painstakingly in order. In her tears and whaling the night before she expressed the hassles of the Colombian bureaucracy. It didn't matter anymore. We could get married! We had forty-eight hours to validate the certificate! Our beginning, like every beginning, lay before us.

Now we have a little chuckle about all this, but the way things had been arranged down to the hour, there was no room for error. Planning and filing forms is something I'm good at. We still had the actual green card to file. The papers I had already prepared were an inch thick, my divorce papers from previous marriages thirty years before, my tax statements from the last three years, my birth certificate, the mailings of requests for original documentation, the exact combing of every line of every last detail.

I had checklists and even created a mockup duplicate of the entire legal mountain of paperwork. I know my training in my second Masters in computer science seriously honed my stills, and developed my ability to get it exactly right. I don't trust anyone to do my work, so a lawyer was out of the question. I had heard a lawyer was more trouble than they are worth and that the papers filed by individuals were considered before the law professionals. The marriage license was only one of the many documents; the actual marriage certificate would come a few weeks later. I had to make sure I was aware of the timing of everything.

Can someone please forgive me for being out of character and see I was under tremendous constraints? Thank you.

The day before the wedding we had a rehearsal and dinner. My best man Sandy and his wife Eileen attended it. Flor, Diana's maid of honor was there with her son. The minister, Lilia, and we two love doves attended. We rehearsed through the positioning and the music. Our vows were practiced. The ceremony was put together from a ceremony outline and a collection of writings from a Unitarian Universalist handout. Lilia, and myself, are of this denomination. The dinner and rehearsal went without any snags. Diana went home with Flor so she would be able to get her hair and makeup done before the wedding.

My two friends had come from Oregon and Denver. Steve is my best friend from high school. I lived with him and his family when I left my parents house because of the violence toward me. Jan is my long time friend from Denmark. Jan was currently working at the university teaching Danish in Oregon. I met Jan on a bus to Amsterdam some ten years ago. We sat next to each other on an overnight bus and have been good friends ever since. I was deeply honored by both friends having come to see me get married. My best man made an extra effort in that he came from Manhattan two days in a row. I've known him the least amount of time, and appreciated his friendship and mentoring while we discussed my relationship with Diana.

It was time for me to catch up with Steve and Jan. We sat around talking and exchanging stories. Steve is like a brother to me. We played in a rock n roll garage band and lived every moment of the British Invasion together. He loves to bring up my shortcomings, but this time he seemed to give me all the support and respect I needed. Jan is like a Buddhist monk. He quotes Kierkegaard and has given me an education on the Danish philosophers. He pauses before he speaks and never says anything negative about anyone. Both of my friends have seen me through major crises at different times in my life. Steve stayed at a local hotel. Jan went to my good friend's Victoria's house for the night.

The wedding day my two friends were at my door early and we set up the wedding in my backyard. I placed a large designer rug on the lawn for the wedding party to stand on. Above, from the trees, I had two strands of flags from Central and South America. These had been in my classroom, but the fire Marshall had me remove them because they were a "fire hazard". I was putting new use to a discarded educational tool I had to begrudgingly remove. Additionally I had some Hindu and Buddhist batik flags stretching directly above our heads. I carefully built a shrine. The small table was covered with a Muslim prayer cloth. I placed various deities, flowers, and candles amongst Diana's Catholic relics.

The yard was beautiful and full of color. We set some speakers out, laid out two rolls of unmatched chairs, brought potted plants from the landlord's son's house, and set up some borrowed tables for the dinner that was to follow. Around ten o'clock we took off to go buy the flowers from a wholesale garden shop. Four, or five-dozen pink roses divided into small glass vases and paper tablecloths from a Dollar Store all arranged in order, transformed the yard into a ballroom. We also purchased a few bottles of wine and some beer. The hour was drawing near and we had to get dressed. Two o'clock was the deadline hour. I kept in motion to stay focused.

I think I own two suits. I wore a double-breasted suit a customer had given me while I was his driver ten years passed. My shirt was from a discount clothing store. This was the only new thing I wore. My shoes I had given to me years past from another customer when I was a chauffeur working my way through my Masters program at the University. For me new cloths are never as good as my favorite cloths, usually something someone has given me. I believe the energy of others is in their gifts. Victoria who had come to lend a hand a few hours before the event made the bouquet and buttoner. She gave the final approval for the settings and placements.

My cousin Eileen is a successful writer. She and her husband Sandy, the best man, drove in from Manhattan. Eileen had just published a cookbook. She had cooked a meal fit for kings and queens from her cookbook. I'm serious; the food was better than anything in my memory. She also cooked the wedding cake. It was cooked with love and from her heart. Sandy had his camera. Two of my previous students were handed cameras, and Jan was on the video camera. Steve had an outline of the ceremony and was the DJ during the service. The nineteen guests began to arrive, some in formal clothes, some in summer shorts and sandals.

I had made the wedding announcements on the computer. They first went out as emails and later as printed cards. Each card was individually made by hand with small artistic borders around a heart shaped design in pink flower petals. In the center was a small photograph of the two of us. The computer was a major reason Diana and I had met. I thought it appropriate to send the good news through the same media first. Later printed cards were sent by regular (snail) mail.

The setting was beautiful. The air was warm and a small breeze wafted the smell of the saltwater and bay into the yard. Birds were singing and the stage was set. The day was slightly overcast. Everyone was there but Diana.

You might think I was worried after forty-five minutes passed the commencing hour, but no I wasn't. Diana stroll around the corner in a gorgeous white dress. (I'm thinking why was this dress inadequate?) She was breath taking and the most beautiful bride on earth. The minister in her dark blue robe called us all to stand. Flor read Kahlil Gibran, Sandy read a quote from the bible, and Eileen read a few lines by George Eliot. Lilia, the minister, read and spoke the ceremony in her thick Colombian accent. The ceremony was in both English and Spanish, assigning the languages for separate sections. Nine months and a great deal of risk were about to change our lives forever.

Here is the song I wrote and sang to Diana:

The Wedding Song
by Dennis Cleasby

You are like the mountains,
I am like the sea,
You are always falling for me.

I am like the sky,
You are like the trees,
You are always reaching for me.

Whenever you have trouble,
Please believe in me,
I will give you patience, the key.

To every understanding,
That opens every door,
For you are all I wanted, and more.
Oh my love

As constant as all motion,
As constant as the breeze,
You receive my kiss with gravity.

That holds the orbs in orbit,
That gives a heart full peace,
That causes every moment to cease.
Oh Diana my love

You are all I've wanted,
You are all I've dreamed,
Rainbows crossing mountains with streams.

While everyone is looking,
No one seems to see,
That you and I are traveling in dreams.

That started long ago,
Before infinity,
When angels of God's mercy believed.

That loving is the answer,
Loving sets us free,
To change the course of life and history.
Oh Diana my love

Stars, they burst in halos,
Flowers bloom at sea,
I believe in you and me.
Oh Diana my love, I love you.

We formally welcomed our guests as Mr. and Mrs. Cleasby. The afternoon passed like a wonderful dream. It was a quiet wedding. The music was soft and the nineteen guests milled around greeting each other. No one could get lost in a crowd. It was intimate and honest. No one from either of our families was attending the wedding. The people were there because of love. The sky opened and soon the sun was shining on us all. Is it any wonder?

Chapter 4. The Honeymoon

Our honeymoon was in three parts during the months of July and August. First we went to Washington DC, then up to New Hampshire and Maine, then back to DC and Colonial

Williamsburg. To see the nation's capitol and the abundance of nature is what I thought important to a new bride from a foreign land. The timing of our travel was separated by returns to New York to complete medical exams and send in the immigration documents. By the time we returned home the first time we could send in the legal papers because the wedding certificate had arrived by mail. I timed everything around the quickest possible deadlines to get the book-sized documentation into the government.

In October we went in for the actual interview for the provisional residency. I was caught completely off guard by the interviewers approach and sudden barrage of questions. My thinking was that we were just to pick up the residency card. In some ways this was good to be unprepared. I was open and unguarded until I realized the purpose and seriousness of what was taking place. Diana had studied a list of possible questions and had been preparing, but I never thought I would be the person under the lights. I asked the female interviewer about when we would be separated for the questioning. After the interview, she informed me this only took place when they suspected fraud. I thought this was a common procedure for all interviews. This was a misperception I had, probably from watching too many movies. We showed our wedding and honeymoon albums. The interview shifted when Diana and the woman began to speak in Spanish. About midway through the woman said she was granting the residency. The tone in the room was very friendly and comfortable. My original feelings of being interrogated passed into a relaxed flow of stories about myself, how we met, and my travels to Colombia. Never lie, it only makes things worse.

The day after our marriage we spent with my two friends Jan and Steve. The four of us drove into New York City and went to the Metropolitan Museum of Art. I remember being irritated by security for not allowing us to videotape on the rooftop sculpture garden. We did get some still photographs in. What is the difference between still photography and video? The sun was glaring and the heat was delicious. I was with three of my favorite people on earth. In the afternoon we went to Little India and found a favorite restaurant. Jan politely, in his totally non-aggressive manner, brushed a cockroach off his shirtsleeve. We then noticed the walls had many tiny visitors eyeing our food. We all lost our appetite and the restaurant lost a repeating customer. That night we four sat under the trees in the backyard and enjoyed the leftover wedding food. The day went like the best of days. Precious goodbyes followed the next morning at the airport when we dropped off Jan. Steve had already returned his rental car that morning at a different airport. I was at last alone with my new bride. We went home to catch up on doing what newlyweds do.

The rest of the day we packed the car and a small suitcase for a trip to Washington DC. What better place than the nation's capital to show a new bride from a foreign country. The five hour drive went fast and we soon found our budget hotel, which I'd booked online a day before. After organizing the hotel room we went out to see the monuments at night. The first stop was the Lincoln Memorial. We arrived just after sunset. It was hot and the people climbing up and down the steps looked like dark ghosts. The white marble of the structure, and intense lights gave everything an air of immense heavenly calm. The large crowd was quiet and I remember thinking how it was that so many people were in a mood of respect. No one was yelling or acting-out. We all knew how good it was to be Americans. There was a calm expression on all the people that was good to see.

We soon drove over to the Jefferson Memorial where there were less people. It was not as accessible and we walked a long distance to get there. At times the path was in total darkness. I remember years before when a car was allowed right next to the site. Now, like so many other parts of American life, the memorials had been separated from the people. Barricades and security was now the precedence. Protection seemed more important than sharing access. My country has changed and my new bride knows nothing of the way we used to be. The people are the same but now the isolation of what was the people's property has become the property of the elite and powerful. I resent this rape of my heritage. To preserve old monuments is one thing. To fortify them and keep them away from the common people is a loss of the true values of freedom and democracy. Some of my thinking I was able to express to Diana. Some of my words were misunderstood. We still barely knew each other.

In the morning we got up and walked to the bus stop where we took a local bus to the National Mall. We were the only white folks on the bus. Diana has a way of endearing herself to people and being open. She noticed how angry and down the bus passengers looked. They didn't have a honeymoon to enjoy. Most of them were going to work and filled with the drudgery of day-to-day life. Diana had her first taste of the other America we seldom see or hear about. The poor conditions of the houses in the run down neighborhoods, the rough look of the passengers, and the weakness of unfulfilled hope all changed in an instant as we entered downtown. Like passing between a dead zone and into a movie set, we disembarked and walked on concrete sidewalks that had no cracks. The curbs were perfect and small manicured parks with golden statues to long passed war hero's had dotted our path to the Smithsonian. I had the video and still cameras, recording everything but the invisible poverty a few blocks away. "How can this be in such a rich country?" Diana said in perfect English as we rode the bus.

We walked along Pennsylvania Avenue to the National Museum of Art, crossed the street and entered on the opposite side of the building near the Mall. The artwork and atmosphere of the museum lulled us into a slow walking pace. There was nothing to do but enjoy our visual senses. We saw the four Thomas Cole paintings on the journey of life, the Rembrandt Galleries, and my mother's favorite painter, Jean Baptiste Camille Corot. I could feel my mother with us. I wanted to impress Diana by calling out the names of the artist before we could see the title plaques. I was in my element. The peace inside the paintings spilled into the walkways like air near an ocean. We held hands and hugged like two school children. At noon we took out the lunch we had packed. We sat in the underground cafeteria of the museum eating and giggling.

The Museum of the American Indian was second on the list of places to see. My fascination for the first peoples of my country has never evaporated since my childhood. We looked at the jewelry and hand weavings with equal intrigue. When we came to a room with a wall of Pre-Columbian gold, Diana instantly jumped with excitement. "This is of my country!" A huge spiraling mass of gold filled a wall behind glass. Now we were seeing something real, not foreign, but from her homeland. I was happy for her. This was my second time to the museum. Unfortunately, during my first visit with my students, we were told to leave because of an unruly student was making a nuisance of himself. I had to take responsibility for one student who wasn't supposed to be in my group. We sat outside for an hour and waited for the rest of the school tour. This time I could see the entire building and every graceful curve. There isn't one corner or square in the whole building, only the circle of life.

The Botanical Gardens was our next pleasure. I was busy taking pictures and feeling no pain at discovering a new friend. I promised myself that being married this time was going to be like a walk in a garden. A small room of orchids seduced us. The low light made it impossible to get a clear image. I was keeping true to my record, take one good photograph and twenty bad ones, but keep shooting. In the rain forest pavilion we lost each other and I saw Diana from an overhead lookout. It was the first time we had drifted in separate directions.

That night we rode the bus back to the hotel. The crowds of working commuters seemed more hospitable than the midmorning crew. Diana always thanks the bus drivers. The walk was in an empty neighborhood with warehouses. We didn't mind because we were safe. The hotel lobby was full of Japanese tourists. The room was waiting. We had dinner in the room, Bohemian style.

The second day we saw the Aerospace Museum and the Museum of Natural History. It was a weekend and more people came and went on the Mall. The bus ride in and the constant pace of walking all day caused us to tire, so we took many pauses and shared park benches. The heat was stronger than on the previous day.

As I wrote before, we drove back to New York and received the marriage certificate by mail. The last document for the immigration and residency had come in. A medical exam was set up with a nearby doctor. We waited one more day for the Aids tests results, picked them up and sent in four months of planning and exact line for line preparation. All the hurtles were being jumped on time and within budget. One screw up could set our plans back by months. I made checklists and placed them on top of each separate filed packet so the checklist would obviously be seen first. I wrote five checks and sent out five packages. Diana's arrival, the marriage application, the wedding, and the papers were all behind us within a few crucial weeks. Just like a flower our life together was beginning to bloom as we finished all the responsibilities of the paper chase. There weren't any more outbursts coming from me. I was getting better at understanding her English, and better at getting my Spanish across.

We left for New Hampshire and Maine after a few comfortable days back home on Long Island. I'd joined Kamp Grounds of America (KOA) and we found our camp after a seven-hour drive north. We were a few miles south of Littleton, New Hampshire. As we walked the small town I realized I'd seen a TV program about the economic turnaround and new tourism that was taking place. It was a beautiful slice of Americana and perfect to show my new bride what my country was like in the inner heart. We found shops with all the fine touches that come with pride in ownership. The worlds longest candy counter was across the street form the public library. Hippie shops with crystals, incense, and chimes are a favorite of mine. We bought a batik of the seven symbols of the Chakras. It was black, with the symbols in bright colors.

We pitched the tent on a wooden platform near a small creek with the sound of flowing water and the fragrance of pine tress. We had cots and thick blankets as well as sleeping bags. I purchased these items for Diana before her arrival. The car was full of provisions, a cooler, and our bicycles. These things had to be unloaded and organized. We had enough clothes and supplies for a year, not three weeks. I built a fire and got the beds ready for the night. Storms were in the forecast. And that it did.

By morning we were warm in our separate sleeping bags. The rain had come in and we found a puddle of water, or a small pond, at our feet. Some of the clothes had become like a sponge and we had to find dry clothes. We used most of our towels to sop up the water on the floor ringing them out and returning to get the rest. Our honeymoon teepee was a wet swimming nightmare. Diana took things in stride. It was the first time in her life she had slept in a tent. We were happy to be facing new challenges together.

We went to the local discount warehouse and bought some water proofing liquid for the tent seams. The morning drizzle stopped by the time we returned and I went about waterproofing the tent. All excess clothes and bags were removed from the tent floor. The stream was louder from the rain the night before. I thought being on a platform would keep water away. No it didn't. We got the camp organized and went off searching for interesting things to see. We drove to the Sate Park and walked to see the "Old Man of the Mountain". We were baffled. I have a good imagination but I was darned if I could see any face in the rocks. Soon some other vacationers came by and explained that it had fallen down that winter. The old man was gone. I felt relieved and sad at the same time. At least I wasn't crazy. Erosion and natural deterioration of the land had taken our friend the winter before. The trail markers and path hadn't been updated yet. Funny, but true.

Franconia State Park was on the map, so we headed there. We parked the car and took the shuttle to the trailhead of this amazing natural attraction. We asked Hasidic Jews and Indian immigrants to take our picture. The sound of the waterfall in the small notch was like a screaming train. It wasn't easy to have discussions with anyone so we motioned for a photograph with our hand, pointing to the camera. We saw the first covered bridge built

in New Hampshire and read the story how a fisherman named
Franconia had discovered the Notch. This was a moss covered rock
with a rushing river between two tall, very tall, walls of granite.
We returned to the car and drove to the town of North Conway.
The restroom at McDonalds was put to use while the line of traffic
went as far as the eye could see. The construction while widening
the roads made the small town a traffic disaster.

Our second night in the tent was much better. The rain
came in but nothing like the night before. It was manageable and a
few minutes later we finished mopping up and were eating our
breakfast. We walked to the showers and struck up a conversation
with a camp worker. I innocently said my wife was from Colombia
and the man made a joke about drugs and suitcases of money. I
didn't think that much of the passing comment. He thought he was
funny. Diana was livid and I listened to her anger for a few
minutes. "My country is the best in the world, we are not just about
drugs." This was her defense and not so much spoken correctly, as
well understood by the time the topic shifted. It did come back
many times that day and ever since. I tried to explain the man was
only making small talk to be friendly, not foisting discrimination
on her. Jokes that point out people's differences aren't so funny to
the unwilling recipient, only to those who want to feel superior.
Being the brunt of a joke is sad. This was the first time I noticed
that the subject of immigrants, those "other people" was discussed.
The man lumped Diana in with the illegal migrant workers in
conversation. A lack of exposure to people south of the border is
the only justification I can think of. What I took as ignorance
Diana took as a full-blown insult. Prejudice can be quickly hidden
and seemingly erased if passed off as a joke.

Just over the border in Maine we visited some long-time
friends of mine. Years before I had spent some time in a small
town named Weld. I knew several people there. I'd begun
vacationing there with a man who had a small cabin. Often I was
given permission to go up by myself and spend five or six weeks
during the summer. The cabin had no electricity or running water,
but I loved it. I had the radio on NPR and spent my time painting

and playing my guitar. A small community art gallery opened and I did musical performances and had art shows. The art gallery was a converted barn. The owners lived in the attached house, which has a general store on the main floor. It was called Milford's Gallery, after the horse that had lived and died in the barn. The owners have since become born again Christians and withdrawn from the business of art.

My friends Jane and Pete have been close for years. I met Jane on the waters edge one summer day. Her sister, Phoebe, approached another musician and I. "Do you guys have a capo for my sister's guitar". We brought the guitars over and thus began years of a musical friendship. Pete and Jane got together after Jane's husband left her for the sister in law. So goes life in small towns and everywhere else. I am an honorary member of the family. I can drive to Maine anytime and know I have a second family. The truth is I'm closer to them than my own siblings. Both my parents have passed and my familial relationships are only alive with one sister. A riff has been going for thirty years now because I divulged my sister's sexual abuse by our grandfather to our aunt (his daughter). Sides were taken and to this day denial has separated us. Sweeping the dirt under the carpet is a family tradition.

I called the week before and asked if we could pitch the tent in their backyard. This time the bathroom and shower were a few feet away inside a warm house. The next week we went on some road trips to the shore and saw some local attractions. Diana saw her first State Fair, livestock exhibitions, and all. We had our photograph taken under the giant wooden statue of Paul Bunyan, the mythological lumberjack from Maine. Twice we drove over to Arcadia State Park and lay on the rocks where the pounding surf crashes. Jane's dad lives next door; in fact, the entire family live within a mile of each other on plots of land, some adjoining, some down the road a piece. Tim is Jane's dad. He is out of a page in history. He grew up on a farm up the hillside when the valley had thousands of inhabitants. His family was bare-foot-poor. They had lived through the depression and kept each other warm in the winter by piling three or four children into a bed. He came from a family of twelve. His mother died and his father married a woman that took care of the children like they were her own. This woman was a painter. I've run into her artwork here and there.

Her name was Janet Dexter Storer. The first time I saw one of her landscapes I knew this was a talent. Her paintings are hung in the local historical society. Somewhere between changing diapers and feeding an army of children she found the time to be creative. Her art has deeply impressed me. The paintings are of landscapes, my own love, and scenes of the area. Tim would tell us stories of the old days, as I'd look at her paintings in the kitchen.

Before Jane's mom died I did a musical performance at the home she was living in. Through casual acquaintances I met another musician named Jim. Jim lived in a cabin, which was way off a dirt road deep in the woods. He made birch bark baskets in the style of the American Indians. I had him teach me how to make one. I still own it. We played music with another man named Jim from New York. Our performances at Milford's and the local State Park quickly made us friends with the locals. The three of us would sit up late in the night with Pete and play music. Jane's job as a corrections officer caused her to retire early. It was a heavenly time full of promise and good stories. We would laugh ourselves to sleep in the large room above Jane's garage. The x-husband had never finished the room, and a broken Jacuzzi sat in the middle, but we had a dry floor and sleeping bags to keep us warm. The wood stove was used on cold nights and we'd write insane silly songs to play at our gigs. When I showed up with my new bride both of my friends named Jim had long passed into stories and I was the only one who kept coming back. Why people lose touch with each other is a strange sad situation. We have all this technology for communication, but don't keep in touch.

Jane and Pete welcomed us and the rest of the family drifted in from day to day. There is no formal time. The door is always open. We could be around back near the fire at night, or in the kitchen. Eventually we saw everyone here or there. I was there when Cassie, Jane's daughter, had her first child. I made a video of the baby in the hospital. I sent it up to Maine for them to have a record of this tiny miracle. Billy, Cassie's husband, works with his dad as a house painter. Cassie and Billy moved away to Florida for a few years but came back to Maine. My friends in Maine remind me of the friends I had in Nebraska when I was living there. We never called ahead to see if someone was home. If a person called, they were strange and a bit off. Spontaneity was the only real way to live. Being formal was too "suburban" for our revolutionary way of life.

Diana made a big hit by cooking some Colombian dishes of beans and rice. Diana wanted to find family and she did. "My friends in Maine are like the people of Colombia" she commented then, and many times since. The simple unpretentious life is healthy for the soul. No one is competing. The beer consumption is a bit excessive, but sitting around a nightly campfire tends to lend itself to such relaxed consumption. The harsh winter weather leaves it's mark like a ring on an old bathtub. Things sit in the yard for months and before you know it they have been there for years. The house and barn have a stain as high as the snow drifts lay that year. Why paint when the winter always wins.

One uncomfortable mannerism of Diana is to tap me on the arm as I drive. At first I took this as a very aggressive gesture. I tried to mimic the behavior back, but she didn't seem to mind at all. As I would drive I would be tapped and cajoled. She would do this to get her point across. It drove me crazy. We didn't have a perfect honeymoon, but not because of some spoiled middle-class discomforts. We are both older than most newly weds. There were times I was short tempered. Diana talked more than I; she didn't listen as much as spoke. I was in constant listening and interpreting mode. For me this is not a casual exercise. For Diana the same was being felt but not said.

One day I took Diana up a dirt road between two mountain passes that seldom had traffic. I stopped the car and asked her to sit in the drivers seat. She reluctantly agreed. She drove a little while and was doing ok. The fastest she went was seven to eight miles an hour. Then I showed her reverse. She went back a little and I tried to show her how to turn while in reverse. I helped her make the turn into a side road. We went straight again and I told her to speed up. She began to go a bit too fast. Then I began to panic. "Stop, put the brake on! Stop!" I remember looking at her face. She was laughing hysterically as we drove off the road propelling the car over rocks and into a line of shrubs. The only thing that kept us from turning over was a large boulder that tore through the front bumper and under-chaise. I was screaming, "Stop the f----ing car!" She was crying, full of fear and weeping like a baby. I waded through the bush looking for bumper and plastic parts. This is a good example of how not to begin driving lessons. Diana had never sat in a drivers seat let alone drive a car before. The trauma of that day has probably saved our lives and caused a deep enough fear that the scar has left a lasting mark. It was months before she would get behind the wheel again. We did in the beach parking lot months later.

I've had to correct her version of the story and remind her that the front end of the car would not have been damaged if we were driving in reverse. I think she only remembers the driving in reverse part. The rest is an understandable blur. This is the second time she openly admits to hating me, and wondered what she was doing in such a disastrous marriage. I've since helped pay for driving classes and tried to figure out why I'm such a fool. Pete helped me pull the car up on some rafters and we secured the lose undercarriage. My tail is still between my legs, in reverse.

I'm not immune to making mistakes. I will make more. I don't like even thinking about some of my poorer qualities. A few days before we left, I wanted us to climb a mountain. Pete told us it was an easy trail. We did reach the summit but Diana was near exhaustion. She slipped and bruised her butt on the way down from the top. What I thought would be a few hours casual strolling was six hours of strenuous hiking. My wife was getting used to a real idiot. She has told me since that she was ready to return to her native country, and I believe her. Usually a honeymoon is just that. I've tried to make it up to her. I had no idea what I was putting her through. In some ways I can never see it from her side. She loves me and we both keep giving, but we hike on casual, safe trails now.

We spent many nights snuggling up in the tent and didn't get up until well after Jane and Pete had gone to work. The house and huge yard was ours to play in. Behind the house are logging roads that lead back into the woods. We'd see Tim across the two yards in his bib overalls. He'd walk with his cane in one hand and a cigarette in the other. He'd be doing some chores and followed by his old dog, step for step. The smell of pine trees and the occasional yawn of a passing car on the dew-soaked pavement added to the peaceful isolation that dripped into our souls like maple syrup. The slow pace of life caught up with us, only to be reminded that home on Long Island was waiting. We said our goodbyes and made the nine-hour drive back home in one day.

For the next few days we entertained periodic guest at our home. My friend Victoria came one day and two of my former photography students came over for lunch. Many an afternoon was spent with company in the backyard enjoying lunch. We had two and half weeks until I began to start teaching again. I was getting restless and we decided another road trip would be fun. Out came the camping gear and we found a KOA outside of Washington DC. After the five hour drive we pitched the tent and went to sleep. The next day we took the metro into the capitol to revisit the National Mall. Most of the day we were walking in the new Smithsonian Art Museums. We'd bought a special day pass so we had to return by five o'clock to the train. In the night we drove to a modern multiplex cinema and saw a comedy. The mall was full of youngsters walking around like they owned the entire earth, full of themselves and not aware of any other people on the planet. Diana said she felt like E.T. By now we were getting used to each other's language. Having fun became our priority.

We booked another KOA in Williamsburg, Virginia and saw the colonial sites. We pitched the tent in an isolated sector of the campground. The bugs at night were loud and our sleeping was very comfortable. The next day we drove for an hour and stayed in a KOA outside of Virginia Beach. That night we bought some souvenirs, listened to a concert of classical music, and walked on the waters edge looking at the lights along the boardwalk. Diana held my hand and told me she loved me. I was the best husband in the world. As we walked in the water I didn't want the summer to end. We are still reliving the good parts, and like a blessing, we forget what was ugly and stupid. We were sharing new territory, new friends, and beginning to understand why we had both made such a leap of faith.

Chapter 5. Culture

Culture is the thin skin we all wear to identify what is familiar and comfortable to us. Deep inside we all bear the same genetic code, we all have the same African ancestors, and we all suffer, laugh, and bond with our families and friends. We are all conditioned to believe that our culture is the best; without exception. But beyond this thin veneer of behavior we are common to all our brothers and sisters. So why all the fuss?

Our marriage is obviously of two different countries, but in an odd way also two different times. My family life in the early 1950's is very familiar to the Colombian way of life today. The focus is on the family and friends. Without great material distraction people can enjoy each other and seek out the elemental truth of life that comes with sitting down and breaking bread. We use culture to either reinforce or blame any given situation. Sometimes culture is a badge of honor, other times the curse of ignorance.

I attended a wedding party in Bali, Indonesia once. I had to walk almost a mile up a steep hill to a house that we in the Western world would constitute as a shack. There was no running water; this had to be carried up on the heads of those who needed it. Along the winding path were occasional houses and barefooted children laborers. The children were carrying large stacks of bricks up the incline on their heads. The house had chickens and dogs that were almost considered extended family. The dogs lived in the house. The wedding went on for several days. I was there on a day when the guests paid tribute. Each guest was to bring a gift and show his respect to the bride and groom, as well as the parents of the groom who's house the newly weds were about to live in. The food was full of flies. The babies had runny noses, and flies buzzing around their faces. The people smiled as if I were an alien from Mars. I was an honored guest. My gift of cash was meager, but my attitude was one of respect and delight at being invited. They all sensed this as we sat on a mat, crossed legged, eating and drinking a clear, home made, liquor that tasted like gasoline.

I had become friendly with a driver I'd hired from the local village. He in turn introduced me to his cousin who was having the wedding. The village was in a fishing community that had three oceanfront hotels; recently built. Because of depleted fishing stocks, only half as many fishing boats were being used. These beautifully decorated boats were the pride of their owners. Status was associated with having one of these vessels. Early in the morning, before sunrise the men would board their crafts and head out to sea. The horizon would be speckled with lights like stars in a long line while their kerosene lanterns indicated the quantity of men using nets as their grandfathers had for many years before.

My new Balinese friend had told me how he had an Australian girlfriend who had bought him a boat. But because of Japanese corporations fishing the waters, the stocks had been so low that he seldom took the boat out. His livelihood depended more on meeting female tourists and wooing them on the beach for sex and money. At the wedding I met his wife and child. He had kept this bit of information from me until another relative introduced his wife. I knew I was on the inside of the family circle when he explained his business was separate from his family. He neglected to tell his wife all the details and appreciated my silence on the matter. I didn't speak her language anyway. But I was aware of a typical male characteristic; to hide philandering is universal and disgusting in any culture. Hispanic men are known for similar traits.

Diana has a very high image of her culture and country. She is quick to compare the short comings of the United States and extol her own nation. In the United States we pay a heavy price to have all the material comforts. That price comes as alienation and isolation from the community life that other nations have in their day to day life. I have seen enough of the world to know that the quality of life is very different anywhere else but the United States. Her view of a society wound like a clock is accurate. The homeless on the streets are a subtle side-show that is never center stage and kept in the category of "unfortunate", but isolated from the mainstream. In the soul of the Unites States power and might there is a cancer that is treatable, but never addressed except with a bandage of occasional legislation. The pace of the race is more important than the runners. My early artistic life in the counter culture gives me the ability to criticize with distain the rigidity of conformity. I see myself as an internationalist and global citizen. I know I am somewhat ethnocentric and bare the burden of being an "American". My trips to Costa Rica and Colombia have educated me to learn that everyone in this hemisphere is an "American". I'm really only a North American. And really, I'm only a member of planet earth.

I know what it is like to be thrust into another culture. On the surface it means that customs and behavior are different. I experienced this so many times that it became a kind of awareness to details, not an obstacle to my survival. The game of life is adaptation and adjustment. If you are stuck in your culture, in this day and age, you'd better get used to the constant shift of life's circumstances. I can't give an answer as to if it was better in the past, or if the globalization of American culture is going to make the world a horrible nightmare. I know it's happening and we are in the middle of this global, cultural dynamic that is tremendous.

In the United Sates we are accustomed to the multicultural influences. For thirty years (plus) we have been inundated with huge Hispanic influences, mostly in places like New York, Texas, and California. In New York we have so many cultural neighborhoods that it makes the city fun and exciting to visit. We embrace the new influences like a trip to Disneyland. I'm not saying there isn't racism towards Black and Hispanics. For traditional African- Americans life is a struggle that is unjust in such abundance of wealth. I know some people judge Diana from her accent. She looks Hispanic or Middle Eastern. She has told me about the subtle distinctions she's observed. I've seen how impatient strangers can become when she is speaking and they don't fully understand her accent.

Sometimes I feel like culture and religion are the two biggest stumbling blocks to progress in the world. My attitude about my own culture is that it needs much improvement, but I don't come from a long-term deep tradition. My reference of culture isn't singular. Yes, I'm "Irish", and "Italian, and "German", but I was always an American first. That meant being in the constant, changing stream of modernism, experiencing the changes as they happened, so much so that there was nothing to hold on to in my past. The expectation of new and different experiences was more a part of growing up "American" than identifying with a way of dancing, a type of cloths to wear, a food to eat, or traditions. So can I fully appreciate a "culture", not really. My old fashioned Irish grandmother (second generation) wasn't Irish so much as a person that represented staunch conservatism mixed with a slight ting of bigotry towards dark skinned people. In her eyes people's good character was always overshadowed by their separate religious, social, and ethnic identity. I never understood this, and saw it as false pride. I'm sure this has effected my view of Diana's change into American life. It's a fine line between arrogance and pride.

Food is a big part of all cultures. Hot dogs, more specifically chicken dogs, are not sausage. Why is it so difficult to know this? Now I know it's not great for diplomacy to begin with the topic of food on a negative note. I need to explain that our house has been a potpourri of exotic smells and fantastic delicious dishes. (How am I doing?) But, hot dogs are not sausage. Hot dogs are a unique part of American life. This is the food of baseball and summer picnics, not spaghetti or rice.

In the fourth month of our marriage I made a direct request. Hot dogs are not sausage. At first this phenomena of creative hot dog use was interesting. It gave the spaghetti mixed with rice a new twist that I thought was something that might become a trend in the North American diet. I began to cringe at the sight of these new and creative dishes. I knew I'd never seen any hot dogs mixed into rice in Costa Rica, or Colombia; these two countries are only separated by Panama, which doesn't use hot dogs either! The only separation I was beginning to wish for was what comes between two slices of bread in the form of a bun. Perhaps my own culture comes out strongest when it comes to my diet. I've spent years trying to fight bad dietary habits that were handed down to me by my parents. I cut out red meat, most breads, and sugar. Coffee is not a part of my diet, and certainly not soft drinks. In Colombia the sausages are the same size as our hot dogs, so my new wife mistook their purpose. Sausages mixed with rice is good, hot dogs mixed with rice is bad!

The portions of food Diana was serving me at first started to add on pounds. In Colombia a mans weight is seen as the quality of the wife's cooking. Food is linked to love and affection. Some of my eating habits Diana plainly didn't understand. She tried some of my raw bran and cereal. She started to take vitamins, but resisted, telling me the vitamins would make her fat. She was soon bloating, full of gas, and constipated from the new foods and vitamins. I honestly didn't realize that her diet was so different that not eating the same foods would create problems. Breakfast in Colombia is eaten with arepas, beans, egg, and a cup of light coffee. The coffee is never black, but as much, or more, milk than coffee. It looks like warmed milk. There is no doubt in my mind that the typical Colombian diet is healthier than the typical American diet. There was some friction between us about the amounts of food, the fat content of the food, and the frying of food. It's not easy to tell your new wife that you think her food will kill you!

What has happened is a cross pollination of our foods. The healthy ones I adopted into my diet. My favorite is an arepas. (The thick flat corn tortia.) Some other foods I eat on occasion, like bunuelos (a round cheese donut without a hole), but know they are fattening and not good for me. I buy chicken sausage now, but still cringe at a hot dog in my spaghetti. A salad is a salad anywhere. It is crucial to get some kind of green, raw food every day. It is easier to do this in Colombia than in the United States. In Colombia fruits and vegetables can be bought at many street corners. Raw fruit drinks are readily available from street vendors everywhere. No, the street industries are not regulated, but maybe the health issues from disease are strongly offset by healthy and natural foods.

In the Latino world gender roles are more defined. In the first months of our marriage Diana would insist on "feeding " her man. She insisted on cleaning the house every day. I mean every day. I feel this should all be a shared responsibility. Living through the sexual revolution and woman's liberation put me in an odd situation where I was trying to liberate my new wife. Diana was raised/trained in the submissive-woman tradition. She thought the woman should cook. I like to cook. She thought the woman should clean. I like to clean. I've been taking care of myself since my teens. A sense of control comes from the daily rituals we create in ourselves. Many of my rituals were put at odds with what role I was expected to play. The transition has been some what smooth, but there were sensitive adaptations to each other's lifestyles. When we go visit friends there is always an obligatory gift of food to be given. The natural instinct to feed others is a common behavior. The minute you sit down in a Latino home the tea, coffee, and cookies come out. Some of these same characteristics are in American life as well, but our tone is less formal, less obvious.

One curious observation of the culture is the separations that come with gender references in language; masculine and feminine words. In the Spanish language everything has a male or female label. The roots of sexism can be embedded into a language. To give an object a gender description is a way to keep the sexes in their distinct roles and forever separate. In that separation men can dominate. In an opposite point of view, the aspect of the Spanish language that uses words towards others as formal and informal can be what keeps families so close. The word "you" has a formal and informal use. "Tu" is an up close and personal word to be used only for family and friends. "Usted" (also meaning you) is a word used for speaking to strangers. If the separation of familiar, and family, are embedded into a language the wall of words can mold a family unit. Since birth Diana's language has always described who was family and who was not. Perhaps this is one reason why Latino culture has such strong family bonds. They truly spend time together. They spend long lengths of time together and the level of congeniality is astounding. The bond is friendly and nurturing. The time I spend with Diana's family is always warm, without pretentious affection, and very enjoyable. I'm learning the language to be able to communicate better with my wife and her family.

To me, the ultimate expression of love is to celebrate what makes us different rather than permit these differences as a wedge. If I can share my identity it leads to better neighboring than forcing my identity on others. The current bickering over the people south of the border will dissolve into history because we are either one human family, or armed encampments fighting wars forever, and uselessly. If you fly a flag be able to fly your neighbors flag as well.

Chapter 6. Intimacy

Why do people get married? Men can never admit it is for sex, woman can never admit it is for security. Well, it's all the above and a lot, lot more. An eighteen year old or eighty year old marry for the same reasons. A mature person has their priorities in order (hopefully), and uses common since. Their sex drive is balanced with emotional needs and physical needs. Thus true intimacy takes place.

I have a theory that people remain together because they are consistent over many years. Problems that were there in the beginning of a relationship remain there, but the coping is different because people mature together. The awareness of each other is also different. Through bonding we trust. I'm not a psychologist, but I've lived enough to know a lot of psychology.

When I was young I suffered an unreasonable amount of physical punishment, at times out and out beatings by both my parents. Years later I joined the peace movement and became ardently opposed to war and violence. To this day I call myself a pacifist. Somewhere between the outer shell of wearing the ideals of Jesus and Buddha, I have violated my own ideals from time to time; I fall short of who I am, or want to be. In all honestly, on emotional levels I've fallen short by being nasty to others, even my new wife. I am glad to report I never beat anyone, like I was beaten. But I still suffer from that state of mind that goes berserk, or in chaos, and wants to inflict pain on others when I'm angry. This is a rare event now, but I know inside I have the capacity to violate another. As I have matured I have seen how my anger leads nowhere except to negative self esteem. Destructive behavior leads me to a cleaning of my emotional house, and seeing I'm not anything like my ideals. The halo and angel wings get trashed, and I feel mortal and stupid. It took me years to make my journey smoother and emotionally comfortable. Smoking marijuana didn't help, but it may have made the creative projects a bit more inventive. Unlike earlier years, I've come to the conclusion that having complete sobriety is the only way to conduct ones life.

I wish when I was being educated the same kind of premarital training were available in schools like today. In the high school where I work there is a program for youth to have a mechanical baby that records the trainees every move. The class prepared students better for real life events in parenting, and equally as important, the depth of responsibility that comes with choosing a partner. My mother asked me if I wanted to know about the "birds and bees" the night before my first wedding when I was eighteen. She actually thought I was still a virgin. What she thought would be a touching and educational moment, equated to an awkward embarrassment to me. My parents never spoke about sex.

To make life an even bigger challenge, I work on a daily basis with kids who come from environments based in dysfunction, neglect, and abuse. I'd say at least seventy-five percent of my students are living in a teenage hell like I did. You'd think I would want to run as far as possible from their problems. But no, I get in there and work the machinery. It is far from easy, and at times I want to punch, kick, and reciprocate as much disrespect as is inflicted on me. As bad as I am, as dysfunctional as I am, and as full of anger as I get, I know I'm pretty damn good at my profession as a photography teacher. The days I get sucked into the mire of student behavior and student dysfunction, I lose. Some days I just stay in neutral to avoid burning out. Some days I don't have enough to give, or spoon feed love to these needy youth. The days I use love as my guiding light, I win, I educate.

I'm no different from my students, I just cope differently. I've revised my attitude. I'm the same person I was when I was young. I'll never let myself forget the bruises my parents gave me. I understand now what kind of chaos my family life was in. I understand my mother's alcohol addiction and my father's rage addiction. I realize enough to undo the past, to know I was powerless over them, and that a great deal of my anger comes from those earlier times. I call myself a "recovery dabbler". I still refuse to accept anyone's authority over me. I've joined twelve step programs and one week with the Hare Krishna's only long enough to reap some knowledge, and still retain my independent heart and soul. There is no one path, except the path I create for myself. That path is full of many influences and doctrines, many teachers, and many good and bad experiences. I came to the conclusion that I was ready to find true love because I understood myself.

True intimacy comes when two people balance each other in tender and loving ways. Sex is the secondary effect, but the weaving dance of real intimacy and sex create an undefined whole. When a man has previous sexual experiences and marries a woman with little or no experiences it is not what most would expect. After any initial sexual "feast" comes the hard work of keeping things in correct dietary control. It's not all dessert, or we become too heavy.

If sex isn't balanced with tender intimate moments of doing small things for your partner, if you think it stays only in the bedroom, I doubt that real intimacy is taking place. Something as simple as a wordless glance in the car, picking up the groceries while leaving the car, cleaning the dishes, making invisible efforts to bring some small comfort to your loved one is a million times more powerful than an orgasm.

The sexual language two people create is nothing less than two people speaking two different languages being put on a desert island. They better start to create a common language, or they will die. No matter whom the people, there is a new beginning between those two. Previous experience can be a hindrance if the expectations are being based on a former lover. It comes down to teaching each other what pleases. The communication in the bedroom is also a reflection of the real day-to-day communication.

The myth of the older man marrying a younger woman for sex is exciting only long enough for the man to realize there will be a learning curve and a great deal of patience required. When we begin new with a partner we bring into the bedroom many other people, maybe everyone we have had relations with. (Which is a justification for people abstaining and not engaging in premarital sex.) If you marry for the bedroom entertainment, it is just that, but not a serious encounter until one faces the task of getting to know, or building a new dialogue with, that individual.

Life has many mysteries and one is sexual pleasure. Sex with love is nothing like sex with strangers. When we make love to strangers we are really making love to our own egos. The depth of emotion that comes with a long-term relationship is a much deeper encounter. There are many shallow brief encounters that take place. But I believe these people are really seeking a deeper meaning in their lives. Before I met Diana I waited three years to let myself go and begin having sex. I was hurt from a previous relationship and wanted to be sure. I was correct in waiting, and healing, before I jumped into anything. The slow friendship that developed on the Internet with Diana gave us the time to build real trust and real friendship. But honestly the real encounter took place after our marriage. One friend said we had a relationship akin to an arranged marriage in India. The sudden pressure to "know" my partner was not easy at times. Explaining the nuances of my sexual needs was not as easy as it may seem. This is a work in progress, and I believe it should always remain that way. Human sexuality is as complicated as individual personalities.

I can't say I always felt this way about sex, intimacy, or even being monogamous. I can't say my path in life is the only way to achieve "real" intimacy. Moral dictates mean nothing. Experiences are what brings maturity, some of us are lucky, some of us die from the risks. The freedom of being able to make mistakes and learn is very important. I grew up in a time of sexual freedom without risk of death, not so anymore. I know that nothing compares to a committed, long-term relationship. I've seen many lonely men seeking a quick fix, and I've been there myself. It's like being an animal more than being a human. Finding moderation and balance is the sane approach to feeding the hungry beast. My life took me to a place that finally embraced abstinence. For me I had to learn that everything worth having entailed some discipline and self-control. There is also discipline in being a successful lover to your wife. The focus should be on giving verses receiving pleasure. The magic comes back around if you are giving to your partner.

In Conclusion this chapter was full of sex; you may have missed it because the subtleties of intimacy were at work. Seriously, understanding boundaries and being a good listener are the key elements to intimacy. The mortar of a brick house is not as obvious as the rows of bricks stacked one upon another. What holds the structure together is the thin, almost invisible, layer of cement. The builders can go as high and wide as they want. The builders never complete the house because they keep adding on new rooms, all the while growing older. Above the bedroom door hangs a sign that reads "Private".

Chapter 7. Language

Most language is really telepathy. How we know what the other person is meaning comes from intuition and reading body language. When the words of a foreign language are present, intent seems to pull you through. Diana's English is weak at this point, but behind a small resource of words is an enormous intellect. She puts sentences together that are very creative and gets the point across, most of the time. What I do is translate the translation.

I am positive anyone else listening to her wouldn't have a clue as to the true meaning of many of her sentences. What is black is white, what is up is down, what is more is "mas", and the mix-up goes well into the realm of the absurd. On our honeymoon there were many conversations that I had to come right out and say, "I don't know what you mean, or what you are saying". It may seem like a huge handy cap, or barrier to communication, but the opposite has occurred.

The sharpening of awareness in listening has become crucial. Despite the typical joke that men and woman view life in such different ways (we do), we also have much more in common than different. Small talk is critical to the ebb and flow of being together. What may have been a conversation a few hours earlier becomes a new conversation when the discussion circles back around. Even though the original language we used was not "correct English", that "incorrect" language still becomes the basis for the recycled topic. The conversation anchors the relationship, correct diction or not.

I found myself speaking in Spanglish, but she wanted me to use English only. I was using a kind of baby talk with an adult; so I abandoned my approach for straight, direct English. I found this helped me feel clear about my use of language, or exactly what I was saying, but I knew she understood only half of what I was saying. I didn't have the computer to help with the translations any more. I felt a little naked. Being face to face created an expected new dimension to our communication, but suddenly a new set of challenges appeared.

As time has progressed, her vocabulary has expanded greatly. The first thing I did was get her out of the house and into a school in my district so Diana would be able to hear English. She volunteered and did small tasks in a classroom with a teacher that spoke Spanish and English. The first two months before volunteering she was in the house alone all day. This would drive anyone used to working and being with their family into a state of insanity. I felt a little guilty for bringing her here to this country and knew I had to get her into a place where she began to function like in her home country. I knew a woman in the school who could help get her into a volunteer situation so I took Diana into the school to meet the right people. They loved her. They, or anyone, can see a genuine person. While Diana was attending the local community college three days a week, she volunteered the other two days. She attended English classes in the college and was learning English in the school. She insisted that I speak only English so she would get better at the language. I reluctantly agreed. My wish to have an in-house teacher was forgotten.

Two months later the school district offered her a full time job as a substitute teacher assistant. She was so personable and consistent that she was offered this better opportunity. I'd finish my job and would wait a half hour to go get her only a mile away. She was full of stories and very excited to be engaged in American life. She is not a stay-at-home wife. I did see a vast jump in her self-esteem, but in all honesty I also saw her occasional depressions. In Colombia Diana was a Speech Therapist and Audiologist. The shock of coming from these prestigious dual careers to being no one in a large place like Long Island was not easy.

I told her how depressed and lonely I was when I moved to New York from Nebraska twenty years earlier. "I was like a foreigner here". She never quite accepted the analogy. The point I was making was how different, and difficult, it is to be uprooted and move away. One's comfort zone is blown completely up when such a move takes place. Every time in my life I moved from one country to another, or one State to another, I went into deep depressions from the shift of my reality. She was no different and all my words couldn't do much more than be a small help.

Selfishly I was thinking, "Most immigrants come here and don't have a husband with a good income to get them through". My own initial entry into Long Island was economic hell. The accents here were something I made fun of, certain words were very comical to me. I came with seven hundred dollars and a broken down Toyota station wagon, full of art supplies. I parked my car in New York City the first night. As I was walking away from the car a passer-by asked me if I was serious. "Why?" "You are actually leaving your car with all those things inside and a bicycle on top?" He said it would all be gone within a few hours. I used twenty-five dollars of my seven hundred to pay for an overnight parking garage. I was hurting already and knew I'd have to get a job fast.

I remember driving the yellow Toyota down one of the Avenues and people waving at me. I was waving back. How could these people know who I was? And why was it most of them were standing on street corners. (I'm serous.) The people waving at taxies saw a yellow car, but my yellow car wasn't the same color as the taxies. I was such a fool, but quickly realized it and laughed. Within a few minutes I had my first finder bender. A big u-haul van bent in my front panel while taking a turn too close. The American Indian driver apologized and neither of us was in the mood to call the police. Soon I was heading to Long Island to find the University I had been accepted into for a Masters in Fine Art. I went from being a big fish in a little pond to guppy in an ocean. I never had the car repaired. I never went back to live in Nebraska, but I wanted to leave New York as soon as possible. That was twenty-two years ago.

All of my major moves came with the benefit of having English spoken where I went. Even in my mid-teens the move to Pakistan included being around people that spoke English. What I've become able to do is easily understand many different accents from a New Yorker, to Irish nuns in Catholic school, to Pakistani English, and to a Colombian wife. I am accustomed to hearing different accents and different languages. If I am at the same table as Diana's family and they are talking I tune out the conversation, but this is something I am able to do if the people are speaking English as well. Diana might ask me if I understood what was being said, but I may just be thinking to myself and not paying attention. I don't sit there feeling left out or that I've missed something.

For Diana I'm sure the shoe is on the other foot and not the same. She feels a great deal of pressure to fit in and pay attention. The amount of effort put into following a conversation is very energy consuming. From an immigrant's side of life, there is a lingering feeling of inferiority, or being second-class. There have been times Diana had objected to me addressing her as my "Colombian" wife. I'm proud of her foreign roots, while she feels I am making her stand out. This is an ongoing work and we struggle with finding the balance. My personality is very casual and laid back; Diana is more proper and conservative.

From my side, the constant listening to her use of English is energy consuming. Do I spend time correcting her English, playing the role of a teacher, or do I just focus on communication taking place. I've decided it is more important to pay attention to what is being said, verses how it is being said. On the other hand, how I say my words can be quite forceful and my tone isn't always good. I don't know why, but I raise my voice when not understood. I know my frustration comes from interpreting what she is saying and putting it into a correct context of understanding. During disagreements this all gets amplified.

Very often her way of saying I understand you is by saying, "You have a reason". I don't know why, but early on during the honeymoon I took these simple words as insults. This could well have been my "baggage", but these words would push my button. It took me many months to see she wasn't being retaliatory, but matter of fact. These kinds of simple misunderstanding can lead to divorce if the partnership isn't focused on love and mutual support. Animosity can begin with a simple word being misunderstood. When there is a tremendous gap as in language differences, it is very important to know every word is not as important as the real tone, and meaning behind what is being said. This may seem easy, but I've found a lot of energy goes into trying to understand what my wife is really saying. This kind of holding back has been a plus to the relationship because I learned to be less reactive and a better listener.

I can see how every man and woman may not accomplish this. If a person hasn't been around foreigners, or different languages, this may seem like an unclimbed mountain. For me it is a creative fascination with how words are put together, and a strong will to succeed at this marriage that has put me beyond ever giving up. Let's face it, isn't it hard enough to figure out what politicians are saying, the truth behind the advertising we watch, and the day to day life of getting along with others in a professional environment when we all speak English? As a teacher, I work with about ten different accents. For me the Haitians are the most difficult to understand. If it is difficult to understand students, it can be equally as easy to shut down and stop trying. This is an honest challenge to life and a marriage when languages are not the same.

Early on I started to keep a log of Diana's expressions that were funny due to incorrect usage. Here is a sampling of sentences and words that she created.

"I no pickeling!" She really means don't tickle me.

"Today I need put water in the hair." I need to wash my hair today.

"Today are beautiful". It is sunny today.

"Today are sad." It is cloudy and grey today.

"You permise me to call my mommy." Do you mind if I call my mother?

"You like come look at the photos of my cirry?" Do you want to see the photographs of my city?

"I doing the cooking." I'll cook.

"You say me look it." Will you look at this?

"You no put ugly. Don't put on ugly." Don't get angry. When I hear this I know I'm being too aggressive and pushy.

"I use it, put one shirt in?" Do you think I should wear an undershirt?

"Come washing the teeth." Let's go brush our teeth.

"Me no like black zipper." I don't like Led Zeppelin.

"I take it, one for one, and clean it." I took them one at a time and cleaned them.

"I think what I go good." I think I look good.

"Are you waiting I have a cancer in the bra?" Are you concerned I have breast cancer? Not so funny a subject, but we had a scare after her first mammogram and they found a dense cyst. It was removed just to be safe.

"I don't clean it this." I didn't clean it.

"No is my house, is your house." It is your house. This is a sensitive issue for me. She has moved into a house that I lived in for five years. I have emptied most of the previous contents only to be reminded that she would live in a house that had very few decorations. I'm a collector. In Colombia the décor is intentionally sparse.

"Today I go to the crackly nut." Today I went to the Nutcracker.

"My stumash is in party." I have an upset stomach.

These are a few of the millions of invented colloquialism she has put out there. To piece together what is exactly being said needs patience, understanding body language, and a will to communicate. Often I have begun to use phrases that only she and I understand. I'm repeating back the "incorrect" language but between us it is fully understandable. Regrettably the more she learns proper English she is loosing her cute expressions. Yes, this is strange, but this is love. What could be worse?

I am dyslexic. It was a surprise discover when I became a teacher at age 46 and attended a workshop on learning disabilities. I knew I wasn't good at spelling and seeing what I was reading, but only at that time did it all fall into place. How I speak, remember information, and process what I hear is often reversed. I laughingly joke that my Spanish is good because in my brain switches around the adjectives and verbs. Spell check is my best friend and computers have given me a new edge on self expression. Because of this "challenge" my life took a creative direction early on. I excelled in art and music (visual and musical creativity) verses the more academic subjects. I liked music and hated math. I compensated my weaknesses by overindulging in my strengths. Maybe the best aspect of this was my ignorance of even having a "handicap" because I was not branded as such. I just knew I was different. Why wasn't important until I matured and sought answers big and small. Perhaps this stumbling block caused me to become a stronger communicator. I love people and love to connect with them. Art, music, and photography always gave me a common ground with any stranger anywhere on the globe. With my wife, learning her language was something I knew I would have to do, and make the best of our situation.

I keep things in perspective by reminding myself there are people who can't even find enough clean water or food to eat. Strip us of everything but our language and we all become very equal. Maybe language evolved in the human chain of evolution so we can tell each other our needs in a more efficient manor. Or maybe our language is non-different from the grunting and groaning of apes. We think we are more sophisticated than animals, all the while acting more savage than all other creatures, because we know the difference between creation and destruction, yet fail to correct the ecological loss of our own heavenly planet. Yes this is strange, but this is life.

CHAPTER 8. DEFENSELESS DRIVING

In the United States driving is a must. Unless you live in a city, ride to work in a boat, or are hospitalized, driving a car is a big part of life. The very invention that gave many people on the planet a set of flying wings is also the invention that may gag us to death by melting the polar caps. Few people on the planet are not aware of what a crucial crossroads we are at concerning the use of fossil fuels. I learned to drive in Pakistan when I was sixteen. My father's driver (every foreigner had to have a driver) took me out in the Volkswagen bus. I learned to drive without my father knowing in a place with horse buggies and men wheeling pushcarts. An animal in the street was as common as a pedestrian. Bicyclists were everywhere. The vehicle had a stick shift, so I was a clutch user from the beginning. I remember few details but I know fear was the basic emotional component during the experience.

I took a Drivers Ed course in high school but never finished the summer driving component. The most difficult part of the class was telling the popular football coach that I wasn't going to complete the driving portion of the course. I had to wait for him in the heat and swallowed nervously as he drove up in the car. I already had my license, so what was the point. Before I had a car I had a small motorcycle. It took me to school and to my job at the steakhouse. I moved from being a dishwasher to a "car-park" within the year. I was getting lots of practice in different types of cars.

I have a long history of driving. In the early seventies I lived in my VW bus and drove to Eugene, Oregon. This was my summer of hippie living. I worked with migrant workers picking apples and pears to have money for food and gas. My brief friendships with other vagabond types set years of musical performance in motion. One man, named Clay, took to me. It may have been that I was alone and in a VW bus, and he was hitch hiking. We met at a crash pad where three or four families were living. I'd plug the electric extension chord into the house and had power for a built-in record player and portable refrigerator. Clay lured me away from the house with stories of easy money up in Washington State. He milked my generosity by buying beer and weed, which he in turn generously shared back with me. We'd park near streams and wash our cloths by hand. I had my guitar and we'd play for other campers in various State parks, going from apple picking job to job. He was tall and handsome with long curly locks. His looks alone would attract attention, but when the two of us played magic occurred. Crowds would gather around us as he bellowed out our short repertoire of songs. I did the harmonies, or played my original songs. Young teenage girls would sit at our feet. When the beer and money ran out, Clay was off to new horizons. I was nearly penniless. Nebraska and my parent's home was the best shelter so I left. I blew an engine rod in Utah and had to borrow money from my father to get home.

By the time I moved to New York (fifteen years later) I had been through many cars and motorcycles. My first was a 1959 Beetle convertible. My second was the VW bus. Gas was seven or eight cents a gallon. I may have had speeding tickets in Nebraska, but I was never in trouble with the law. My first taxi gig in New York was on Long Island while I was a grad student. I hated it. I actually had a customer stiff me once, only to have her get in the car a week later with her boyfriend and two other customers. I never forget a face and let her know so.

I went to a limousine company and the manager laughed at me. "How can a guy from Nebraska drive in New York" I did, and I got pretty good at driving until one month when I got three separate tickets for three separate moving violations. My insurance company dropped me and my new carrier doubled my premiums. That was ten years ago and I've been clean since. Driving in New York City and on the Expressways was tough. I'd sit for hours waiting for customers and waiting for the next job to be called in to me. I had no social life and was trying to make it as a musician and artist; two of the most lucrative professions any middle aged man could dream of. Eventually I quit the limo service and began to do freelance chauffeuring. I did my art and music. I even wrote a weird sci-fi novel on my first Tandy laptop computer while sitting in the cars for hours on end. My life has been inevitably connected to the automobile.

The month I made two hundred dollars, it became painfully obvious that I had to figure out how to get more customers or find another source of money. With my Masters in Fine Art I became a substitute teacher on the days I wasn't driving which would be great one week and bad the next. My income was very very low. I was trying to live like I had in Nebraska, hand to mouth. Being "free and independent" was losing its appeal.

In contrast, my wife has never driven a car. She has been a passenger her entire life. She has lived in Medellin every day of her life and been an avid walker. Medellin is like most cities; if public transportation can't be had a taxi is always there at any street corner. In Diana's neighborhood a one block walk puts her in a city park and immediately into a taxi. The center of Medellin is about fifteen minutes by foot. Diana's first job was a fifteen-minute walk, a short distance from her parents' apartment on the fifth floor of their building. Diana worked at a school for special education with children of varied disabilities. On a visit later I saw her connection to these boys and girls was magnetic. They loved her kindness and sweet manner. Her second job was much further. She would leave the school at 2:30 and begin her second job at 2:45. Diana was a speech and voice therapist for the universities drama department. This job was finished at 7:30 in the evening. I usually called at 8, or close to that time. Every few months she also gave seminars at the university she graduated from. She worked hard and shared her checks with her parents. Walking was a big part of her life that was eliminated when she moved to New York.

After my disastrous first driving lesson on our honeymoon, many months went by before Diana would get behind the wheel. She finally agreed in the local beach parking lot. We began again with a great deal of caution. Each slow turn she took was very slow. We rode in a giant figure eight cycle between two parting lots. I tried to get her to use more speed. I got in the drivers seat and showed her some small circles, giving it a little gas. She began to cry. She was afraid of going too fast. I had assumed wrongly that being a passenger would be intriguing, and an attempt to drive would follow. She thought she would never drive a car. Her father's little white 1980 Fiat was good enough to sit in the back seat. Her mother was always in the front. On weekends they would all drive to see the brother and his family.

Every weekend we'd go back to the beach parking lot. Diana would make up some reason why not to practice. I'd either give her a hard time or go along with her wishes. Much of the conversation then and since, while in the car, has been about driving and what is taking place. The curves, the speed of a curve, the proximity to the curb, and the use of the brake while taking a curve, have all been discussed a million times. This still takes place today. This month she will go for the driving test.

A librarian assistant at my job gave me the driver's education manual and Diana began to study. I got her both English and Spanish versions. I next went online and bought an instructional video. She spent a lot of time studying these in addition to attending her English classes at the community college. She can read English much better than she can write it. Many of her words are pronounced like they are from a book and written. I drove her to get her learners' permit in mid-winter. She missed the first passing score by one, so we returned the following week. She had passed!

On our first visit together to Medellin Diana took driving lessons. Before our arrival her mother had called around and found an instructor that would be able to give her a pre-arranged time slot at eight in the mornings. This was four mornings and four classes. One morning the instructor cancelled so an afternoon class was put in its place. The first morning I stood on the balcony looking down on the street. The class was being given in a mini-van with the schools name plastered on the top and sides of the van. I watched Diana climb into the drivers seat. I waited and waited for them to pull out and drive away. The first class was spent showing Diana all the interior and motor parts and there function. I waited so long I gave up and went inside. They did leave a few minutes before the end of the class. Diana drove around the block. The mini-van had an additional brake for the instructor, but no second steering wheel. Ok, a little different for me, but this was a foreign country.

Diana finished her fourth class and was issued a drivers license. What? I was astounded. All we had to do was go to a clinic and have an eye examination. The results were taken to an office and the license was hers. The driving instructor doubles as a government representative and issues the license. We spent more time waiting in the clinic than she had actual driving time on the street. I sat outside with Tuto, her dad, and we made jokes together as we waited for Diana. After the eye exam we thought that was all, but Diana had to report to the second floor for a test of her reflexes. This was small medical exam of sorts, something else that never happens in the USA.

In the USA the instructor issues no license, and certainly not after ONLY four classes. When Diana went to pay for the classes, the instructor gave her the laminated card. She had to provide a photograph and previously signed the registration papers. Payment was to be given upon receiving the license. Yes, the money was exchanged after the services. Another aspect of life in her country I couldn't grasp. Diana hasn't driven in Colombia other than the classes. The license is an impressive document. The classes were given driving up and down the hills of nearby neighborhoods. Once she was in downtown traffic. She was given the license. Now it was swim or sink. I didn't know if I should be amazed or appalled.

One important note is the strictness of laws in Colombia. The number of traffic police is equal to the number of military police, only to be differentiated by an orange reflective "Traffico" (Traffic) vest. They all wear military uniforms. If the driver of a vehicle uses a cell phone, it is a violation. If the driver is eating, it is a violation. If a person has their feet out the window or exposed on the dashboard, it is a violation. There's no casual funny business. It's all by the book and orderly, if that is the correct word. Don't think this is a sleepy laid-back place where a violation can go unnoticed. There are hundreds of young black-booted motorcycle police who can out run a train. The automatic weapons strapped across their backs gives an extra motivation to comply. I've heard a cop can be bought for such violations and the weekend is an especially popular work shift. I don't drive in Colombia, or Costa Rica. I've rented motorcycles in Costa Rica and had to explain why my New York State drivers' license was back at the rental office, but that's about the extent of my experiences. In Colombia I've seen small fender benders. The speed limit and volume of cars on the road keep the roads relatively safe. Diana has seen car accidents here in the USA. She points out the speed is insane and the real problem.

We began to have Diana drive to our jobs at the school district. The early morning commute was short and few people are on the road at six-thirty in the morning. In the afternoons Diana only drove a few times. In these instructive sessions we often reached a crisis mode. My professional patience as a teacher has mysteriously evaporated. I'm not good. I yell. I scream. I am the worst driving instructor on earth. The worst thing any student needs is to feel bullied. I am my own nightmare and I know it. Using a high pitched voice while instilling fear in a student, in any learning process, is just plain wrong. And teaching driving made me the king of wrong. No matter how I tried I would lose my cool. Some days I'm fine and it goes well. On the bad days I don't respond well to running red lights or running stop signs. I've searched my soul to seek out the source of such unkindness and anger. I'm ashamed of my behavior but I don't know how to always be cool. I noticed some mornings the pressure was already on if we were running five minutes late. I'm a clock freak.

The problem got so bad, and the tearful encounters numbered so many, that we sought help from the minister that married us. Any perfectly quiet, still morning could be transformed into shear fright and yelling. Diana doesn't argue back. This is a trait of her family background. She vents her emotions in the opposite way I do. I was getting pissed off before we even got to the car. I was getting angry about every little thing and every tone of voice. The minister forbad the lessons to continue. I felt the weight of the world removed and within a few days we were beginning to relate in our healthy ways. The problem was still there. Diana needed to learn how to drive. I signed her up for five driving classes and made sure the male instructor spoke Spanish. He was lost for the first lesson and we had to reschedule, but there was some benefit to them. Diana noted the man never yelled at her.

The classes went well, but Diana needed more so I called and got her five more. She is in this process now. The instruction company gives Diana a last class the same day as the road test. If she doesn't pass she will keep trying. The second teacher with this company is a female. She told Diana she had to practice. I reminded Diana that I had been freed of this task, but I've relinquished and have been giving Diana driving practice-lessons in the mornings and in the beach parking lot. I move trash cans which substitute as parked cars and she is up to parallel parking. Her driving is much improved, but I'm a stickler about stopping and counting to four at each stop sign. I have witnessed a strange but common human phenomenon. A person can, within seconds, deny any errors. "I did stop and count to four." Yes, she counted but she never stopped. She touched the brake but she never came to a full stop. This is the same kind of argument my students put forward when I give instruction.

Diana has had lessons from a couple of friends at school. I don't know when the next blow up will come. "You have a reason", is her way of saying I'm correct. (The hard part for me is that Diana is totally dependent on me for all transportation.) Yes I've heard husbands should never give their wives driving lessons. There are millions of stories that warn against such lessons with a spouse. I believe this is wrong to do, to my core, but I also believe in compromise. I know my wife doesn't even always understand the English I am using while I teach. I know this is an effort that is beyond the call of a husbands duty but, will this put my life at risk? Will the vile beast in me rear its ugly head. I am Beowulf. I AM BEOWOLF!

Chapter 9. Ireland

The first trip outside of the United States Diana and I took was to Colombia, the second was to Ireland. We could not leave until we were sure of her residency status and received permission to travel by getting the green card. That Christmas we flew to Arizona to visit a long time friend of Diana who had come to live in the U.S.A. In February we flew to Diana's parent's home in Medellin and spent a week. I thought this was the most important, first trip abroad. After fulfilling an obligation to visit family it was my turn to pick where to go.

INTERNET LOVE: HOW I MET MY WIFE

Diana had received her provisional residency and we were free to travel the globe. Well not exactly. For a Colombian citizen to travel to Ireland, and most foreign countries, a visa is required. Unlike a citizen of the United States who requires a visa for only a handful of countries, Colombians must apply for a visa for almost all countries. The fact that there had been a connection between the Irish Republic Army and FARC (Colombia's guerilla movement) may be a big part of such restrictions. Seven weeks before our departure, we had to send a multitude of documents to the Irish conciliate in New York to secure her permission to travel there. On the other side of the pond my friend of some thirty years, Denis, sent a letter of invitation directly to the Irish conciliate in New York. One of the great luxuries of being an U.S. citizen is our ability to freely trek around the globe with that little blue passport.

Denis and I have a history that is the stuff of books. We met in a boot-making factory back in Omaha, Nebraska in 1972. He and eight other Irish lads were brought into the factory to learn the riding boot trade. I was twenty-one. He is five years older than I. I had been working there for a few months and was the "crimper". I cut out the top foot portion of the leather riding boot, soaked it in a tub of water, and carefully placed it in a hot iron for five to six minutes. In that six-minute window I read books. I read the entire Time-Life series of great artists of the world. I had dropped out of college after one year and was determined that I could educate myself just as well as any stuck up professor. This all tied into an atmosphere of anti-establishment, anti-"the system", anti-everything that was over thirty years old. Actually it made me just as much a conformist as all my other hippie brothers and sisters. I wrote slogans on large sheets of brown paper and posted them on the wall of my working area. I was against the wealthy and all-powerful Capitalist factory owner. Of course this didn't help with my situation, but with my fellow workers, I was somewhat of a revolutionary.

The factory crew was a wonderful mix of longhaired hippies and blue-collar workers. We all mixed with the likes of ex-cons who were there to get a new start in life. In this brew of personalities came nine Irish leprechauns speaking in a tongue few of us could decipher. I was fluent in "Irish" (Irish-English with an accent) because of my Catholic school upbringing, and the fact that my grandparents on my mother's side were first generation immigrants. In Catholic school the nuns could twist an ear, crack a knuckle with a ruler, and spew out a line of angry phrases faster than a drop of Guinness being spilled. As a child I learned to fear their tone of voice first, and later learned the exact words that were being hurled at me in the name of Jesus. I was excited to meet a group of legendary strangers from the land of myth from which part of my heritage had sprung. A group of us (four young workers) waited up until eleven in the night to greet our new coworkers. We had camped in an apartment upstairs from the downtown factory, which would be their apartment, drinking and smoking.

By the time our nine new friends had come off their long airplane trip and up to our rousing reception they were exhausted. We handed them joints and beer as if they would welcome our gestures with open arms. We nearly shocked them to death. These were provincial country lads who went to church and seldom had a drink. They did have a drink, but it was my guitar and singing that seemed to be the real friend catcher. Denis and I have been close friends ever since. A year after he returned to his homeland I was at his door with my guitar. He is my best fan and encouraged me over the years, despite my dwindled aspirations for stardom.

The factor owner had an agreement with the Irish government to introduce a new factory to the (at the time) economically weak country where Denis lived. I have seen Ireland some twelve times over the years beginning in 1965. My parents took the whole family to Pakistan through Europe. Ireland was our first stop. I always pass the same hotel and nearby Bunratty Castle where we stayed just outside the Shannon Airport. I had my first Brownie camera and was fourteen years old. Few of my first photographs were good enough to keep because I thought I had to "catch" the image, like an insect. I shook the camera like I was quickly catching it before it got away. Don't ask me where I got such an ill-directed idea. I have one remaining photograph of a horse in a field. Magically, I also have a photograph my father took of me shooting this photograph while leaning the camera on a post. No doubt my father had given me that instruction. Thus my one good picture from Ireland on my first visit.

My first memories of Ireland were of stark poverty. Other than living in Panama when I was a baby, this was my first exposure to another country after living an insulated suburban life. I saw skinny children in their bare feet and raggedy clothes walking along the small highway. These people were called Tinkers. My parents seemed to lay blame on the fact that they were from a hated class of vagabonds. I felt guilty for being so well off and thought living in a trailer was a very practical way to live. By the time I met Denis, I was turning that guilt into a hatred for the rich and powerful, and writing songs that would change the world. Ah, the energy of youthful romantic idealism. I still live it. I just have to pay bills now. Our family of seven drove from Shannon to Dublin in five days. Everything was totally green even in February.

Years later, so began a life long friendship with Denis. I was living in a small apartment a few blocks away from the factory, but made sure to take Denis to meet my mother. She cooked corn beef and cabbage and had a strange lilt in her voice, as did all of us, after speaking with Denis. The training program lasted six months and we did as much as we could to make our coworkers feel at home. I think one of them eventually smoked some pot, but Denis to this day is as clean as a penny whistle. Well, he does drink. I needn't prolong any Irish stereotypes. Over the years the other Irish workers have died or moved away from County Limerick, and live only in stories Denis and I exchange. There are only two men who remain in our current telephone conversation. We speak at least once a month by phone.

When I told Denis I was getting married, he thought I was crazy. Two summers earlier I had spent over a month as the guests of Denis and Carol, his wife. I was in emotional trauma over a breakup. Denis is the brother I never had. In some ways I am the brother he lost at twelve from tuberculosis. He knows my inner soul, so when I said I was about to marry, he politely asked me what the hell I was getting myself into. They had not met Diana and understandably wanted to never see me relive another bad relationship and subsequent breakup.

Denis has built a home for he and Carol less than a city block away from his ancestral home. This modern home is in the Irish countryside. When I needed a friend, he was there for me. I reciprocated by helping him do the finishing, painted touches on the renovation of his late mothers two hundred year old home. He gutted the house and added a kitchen. The project took him two years. Denis and I are similar when a project is in the works. We are slaves to unfinished projects. We worked together for hours on the house. He counseled me through a difficult time as we worked on the house. I'd work while he was away at his regular day job. For dinners I'd walk up the hill where Carol would feed me. My time was divided between work on the house, walking on the hills, reading books in the sun, and painting watercolors or pastels. I had a very productive summer and we completed most of the house. I attribute my healing of a broken love to my friends and the time alone to re-access my life. Little did I know I was making room in my heart for Diana in the future. At the time I was in pain. Denis listened and engaged me for hours. He prays for me. I chant, pray, and sing for spiritual solace. We attended Sunday mass together. In short he is my best friend and much more.

Denis and Carol faxed me a letter of invitation, not having a clue as to whom I was bringing into their home. When we arrived at six in the morning, a rental car was waiting at the Shannon Airport. We made a few photographic stops. Diana stepped into a magical Irish morning with fog and dew. We went on to the house, had a small breakfast, and went to sleep. No matter how much one tries, the jet lag and time difference is a bomb to the internal body clock. Sleep is the only solution. Diana and I woke and it wasn't long before Denis took me to the side. "She is a gold-mine, so sweet and wonderful." I smiled in return.

Carol and Diana took to each other with equal zeal. Diana spoke in her emerging English and Carol responded in her thick

Irish accent. The first and second days we stayed home. Denis' mother's house down the hill had long been completed and new renters from England were occupying it.

When I go to Ireland, I'd rather stay home more than anything. Behind Denis' house is a hill. It is a very large hill (more like a small mountain) that has a stone ruin called Darby's Bed at the top. The ruin is a megalithic tomb of some six or seven huge slabs of stone. From up there the view is spectacular. I've painted this view many times and even wrote a song about the location back on my first visit in 1974. The second day I took Diana to my pilgrimage spot. She was in heaven. Why? The land looks, smells, and feels like Colombia to her. This may seem like a far stretch of the imagination, but the highlands outside of Medellin are very close in appearance to Ireland. The small cars and small winding roads with cattle is a common event in both countries. The hedges dividing the fields and patchwork of colors created in the landscape is also very common. But perhaps the most common thing, is the openness and endearing personalities of the peoples. It is important in both countries to look each other in the eyes, speak from the heart, and be aware of one another on a very personal level. The importance of family and the expression of the Catholic faith made Diana feel like she was home in Colombia. Did I mention Denis and Carol loved Diana instantly?

Denis' son, Graham, is a world-class kayaker. He treks to Norway and Africa looking for rapids. He was away in Africa during our visit. Their daughter, Laura, is a college student studying to be a music teacher. She and I have shared a harmony now and then (while my guitar gently weeps). She makes money singing at weddings and working for a pharmacy on the weekends. There isn't a bad vibe or a course word ever heard coming from any one in the family. I was fortune enough to know both and Denis and Carol's mothers. Birdie was Carols' mother. She passed the summer after I was there last, before I brought Diana. The woman was a saint, soft spoken, and never once in her life uttered a bad word about anyone. Humility and faith lay deep in her character. She was always praying but never made me feel like I was going to burn for eternity like my grandmother, who often spoke to me with distain. Birdie liked me and often sent her greetings via Denis and the phone.

On the third day we took a road trip to show Diana some of the sights. We saw Adair. It is a quaint village with thatched cottages and a grand cathedral. We visited Birdie's vacant house on the way. The shrines to the Virgin were worn where Birdie had kissed them so many times. Over the years the paint was worn away. Nothing has been changed in the house. Graham had stayed there for a few weeks before he left for Africa. Birdie's bed and the simple décor of the house remained still. In each room of the house a picture of Christ with stretching arms greets you. The house was soon to be sold, but for now it was still Birdie's.

One of the most peculiar things to me is how Denis loves to get in the car and drive long distances when he lives in such a pastoral setting. I'm happy to go on a walk, but he likes to put the petal to the metal. Ireland can be driven across in one day. Half the roads are fast highways, the other half are dangerous curving roads with occasional cattle or pedestrians. The high hedges on the sides of the road block any view of future oncoming traffic. At times, the tunneling of hedges on both sides of the road feels claustrophobic. I drive there, but very slowly. Unlike what one would think, I run into problems when I return to drive in the States. I can adjust to driving on the opposite side of the road, but when I come home I have fallen into relapses and found angry New York drivers cursing at the idiot on the wrong side of the road. This takes me a week to get over.

On the fourth day we drove to Shannon Lake, the body of water that lay at the headlands of the Shannon River. The road follows the edge of the lake and we circled half way around the body of water until we were sure we were lost. Denis and I had taken a similar drive a few summers before. We took a Sunday off from working on the house and found this area to be very beautiful. We wanted to show the wives and retrace our path.

Each night of our visit we returned to their house and had a dinner, which included some version of potatoes. Denis is an avid soccer fan so the "tele" was always on when a game was being broadcast. The ladies would talk while doing the dishes. In another room I'd do some artwork or watch whatever from the States satellite news I could find. What a sad statement when Fox news is the only news to be had. The BBC would soon replace that. Eventually we all regrouped for talk or the obligatory guitar concert. The Guinness was out and the friendship was strong, but never bitter like the ale.

After a few days in our guests home we packed the rented car and drove north to spend a few days alone. We headed to Knock, a once small village where the Virgin appeared to a young girl. It was cold and most of the booths selling Catholic souvenirs were closed. We walked into the various churches. Diana felt at home once again because of her devotion.

We then drove to the coast and saw the small town of Westport that hugs the hills at the mouth of a great bay. This section of Ireland is my favorite. It is called Connemara and County Mayo. I love the solitude and colors. On more than one occasion I have been there to sit in the sun and paint the stark mountains with crystal lakes. The vacant roads and sparse terrain give me a great sense of peace. When I go there it takes me into my ancestors lives. I can feel the generations of people struggling in their daily lives, walking an endless road, and searching for a better life to come. That life indeed has come to Ireland. The new prosperity is very apparent. The abundance of traffic on the road into Galway is a sad side-affect of this prosperity. We were heading back toward the city, but the commuters heading home were in a line miles long. There is one road. What should have been a ten minute drive lasted an hour once we hit the center of Galway and found our hotel.

We had a 'once in while' glitch to traveling. The hotel didn't accept my credit card. We had to go find an ATM and pay with cash. There is a new credit card system in Europe where the bearer of a card has to have their photographs embedded in the card. All other cards are not accepted. I've never heard of this before or since, but the rules of plastic commerce are here to stay.

That night we treated ourselves to a real Irish restaurant named McDonald's. We were starved and after parking the car and walking to find an Irish place, we gave up. We gave in. We lowered ourselves to a standard-less fast food meal. The rest of the night we walked the main pedestrian corridor through the city center, looking at the shops and people. The shop windows are like looking back in time. Irish clothes are distinct. The woman's clothes are very old-fashioned looking. The hats are like something out of the funny books. I don't mean to be disrespectful, but I can't take these hats serious. Comical, is the only adjective I can come up with. The mad hatter has visited the green isle and left his mark. I think this is the Irish response to the British upper class. The only time I have seen these ridicules puffed–up displays of fashion in public was at a horse race. Or I see them when a wedding is taking place, but other than that a shop window is the safest place for these visually offensive and jester-like bonnets. The Irish government should out law these hats. Between the small roads, which are a visual handicap, and the large hats being worn by woman driving, the highway death toll could be cut in half if outlawed.

In the morning we drove to more out of the way locations, circling around on costal roads with long views and quaint colorful cottages. I love the colors of Irish houses. The broad window and door trim are always painted with a bright color that emphasizes their shape and gives an accent to a more muted color covering the rest of the house. In the villages, rows of houses are steps from the street and painted in the same attractive manner. Since the economic boom of the 1990's, Ireland has had a fresh layer of paint on every building. The colors are happy. The people are happy. Their temperament is jovial and only in the large cities do you see the sad face of congestion worn by commuters trying to get home. This is very similar to the people of Colombia. Diana will attest to such circumstances.

That same day we had a picnic lunch and drove to the Cliffs of Moher. The once open cliffs are now well protected by guardrails. Despite this, a few weeks before a woman added to the increasing suicide rate and jumped to her death. These cliffs are one of Ireland's incredible natural phenomena. The rocks with crashing surf are so far below the sound does not carry to those listening above. The wind is strong and holding onto a hand is a great comfort when a gust slightly lifts ones body. Diana and I hugged as we walked past a man playing Irish songs on a banjo. A new visitors center has been built. It is underground in the side of a hill in an eco-friendly design. The parking lot is expensive and there is no way to really sit around because all the picnic benches have been replaced by concrete and toll booths. Ah, progress is such sweet smelling money. We had arrived in the late afternoon and had to meet Denis at the Shannon Airport so we didn't stay much over an hour.

The rental car was twice as expensive as we had been quoted when booking it. This isn't a situation exclusive to Ireland. There are always hidden taxes or added insurance coverage's, that in this case, almost doubled the price. Because of this I asked Denis if he would help us drop off the car three days early. The road trip was finished and the remaining driving time would be with Denis in his car anyway. I was sick of being in the car. We had spent so many days in the car that my back went out. The next morning I needed to walk. One of the down sides to traveling is that a car can be a real nuisance and keep one from experiencing the natural world. Watching rolling scenery like a movie is nothing like sitting down and painting it or taking a hike. The same goes when we traveled to Arizona. We spent more time getting to Monument Valley and the Grand Canyon than being there.

The morning was brilliant with streaming sunlight. The smell of blooming flowers and chirping birds was symphonic, so off we went down the single lane to the village of Galbally. Irish spring is not soap. It is a real event in a real place, not a commercial with some stereotypical lady throwing her arms around a sweet smelling, capped hulk. The real smell of cow dung and sheep poop mixed with the fragrances of flowers is an "Irish spring". The cacophony of birds singing can't be packaged. To walk down an Irish lane and experience the wind on your back is truly miraculous. The people passing by have a smile to offer, as well as a small wave.

In the center of the village is a statue of a man holding a rifle. He was one of the liberators from England. This wide expanse of concrete serves as a car park, holds the memorial statue, and is surrounded by a few shops, eateries, a mortuary, and pubs. Two competing grocery stores are a few doors apart. As shoppers stop to go into these tiny markets they double-park. There is still plenty of room to get around them because traffic is rare. The pubs, three in all, are the center of social life, other than the Catholic Church, of course.

On my first visit to Galbally, back in the 1970's, Denis and I went into the pub. Smoke, music, and the sound of laughing farmers gossiping was strong. I recall the event because I encountered a new style of police community relations. At midnight the pub-goers quieted to a hush and the sound of footsteps and a nightstick tapping the door sent us all silently out the back entrance. The Guarda personally know each and every person in his jurisdiction, so a polite reminder of being open passed the legal drinking hour went by with no incidents. As the policeman passed further away on his walking patrol the pub livened up once more, but everyone slowly complied with the order and slipped into the night. "Does this happen every night?" "No, the fools do this once a week, on Saturday night to show they are here", Denis replied. If you go to bed early enough on a Saturday night you can rise early enough to receive the body of Christ on Sunday morning. I was in shock from the civility of the Guarda. Denis had no idea of the Chicago Police riots during the Democratic convention of few years before. I was in Rockford, Illinois, on my way to Chicago when my friend's parents forbad us to go into the city. (Wisely) We stayed home, smoked hashish, and listened to the new 'Doors' album.

Not far from the center of the village is More Abby. This is a stone church with open ceilings. The original wooden ceiling had long passed into history. I lay on the path behind the church while Diana took the camera and did a photographic study of the structure. My back was killing me and lying still in the sun was my only medicine. The abbey is next to a small stream and the pasture between the church and water has a horse, but other than that we were alone. I soaked up as much of Ireland as I could. I knew we would be going home in two days.

We walked home the long way. It is dangerous to walk on the lanes in Ireland. Cars speed at rates that are way too fast. The younger the driver the faster they think they need to go. We crisscrossed the lane whenever we came to a patch that was too narrow to jump out of the way of on coming traffic. Ireland loses hundred of pedestrians every year on these winding lanes. I wasn't about to have Diana and I become a statistic. We retraced our way through the village and took a new road back to Denis' house. When we returned, Denis was cutting his hedge. He stopped, then leaned on the fence as he spoke, like hundreds of other times, he engages in conversation with the local people. The summer we worked on his mothers' house, he often had to stop his progress and address a passer by. I'd keep working and remind him his social skill of gabbing was costing him valuable work hours. Yes, hours.

Diana and I sat in the sun as Denis went back to work. I was on a blanket painting the view from the front of his house. Diana was reading. The Galty Mountains are across the valley and dominate the landscape. These treeless mountains have a patchwork of small pastures at their base. A long, low, gradual sweeping stretch of land causes the eye to read every hedge of yellow Gorse bush. This bush, also called Furzes bush, turns an Irish spring into a bouquet of natural, "screaming" yellow everywhere. The thorny bush was imported to create biological fences, but soon over-took many fields. While visiting New Zealand, I heard a similar story about a much smaller version of the same bush. This beautiful yellow bush has a thorny branch that is the worst natural disaster to every encounter. Hospitalization is the result of a slight misstep. It keeps the cows in the pasture, but it has a beautiful curse. The yellow strands last a few months in spring. This yellow ribbon of color dances up and down every edge of land with bright green pastures between. It is fun to paint and a visual treat of happiness. It is a sign of spring and Easter.

Easter morning we all piled into the car and drove to a neighboring village to attend mass. The priest "said mass faster and gave a shorter sermon", so the extra few minutes of drive was worth it. (I can't make this stuff up. It would be a sin if I did.) The day passed like we were with family in Colombia. Denis never stops working. Carol never slows with stories. And we all prepared the Easter dinner together.

I have to backtrack a little to add a small but important fact to our visit to Ireland. Diana is a devout Catholic. Denis and Carol are equally devout. Diana had heard about the miracles in Knock and wanted to make a special pilgrimage to visit this holy place. We went into one of the many churches and confessions were being held. Diana hadn't been since our marriage and went. I waited outside and said some prayers. I heard a lot of loud talking and thought she was taking a long time. My wife is a saint and doesn't have a long list of faults. I'm a liberated Catholic/ Unitarian Universalist. So I take things in stride, she is more serious. When she exited the confessional she was a bit flushed and very quiet. I thought she was just in a spiritual state and left her alone. We exited the church and began to make our way toward the chapel where the Virgin appeared. I soon saw Diana was crying like a baby.

"What's wrong?" In her tears and thick Colombian accent, "The priest said I was a prostitute." "What?" "He said I was a prostitute and was no longer a child of God because I married you outside of the church." I was floored, and very angry. I had to keep my cool and focused more on treating my upset wife, so we slowly continued walking the grounds and visiting the site. In the car I gave her MY sermon. I may have been too strong, but I had to balance all my skills with careful loving distain for the head-trip she had just received from a stranger hiding behind a curtain. I remember saying, "Your relationship with God should be between you and God first. No one can truly judge that but you." I knew no angry words would help. I told Denis what happened when we got home.

Denis and Carol both consoled Diana on this matter. Denis wanted to know why I didn't go back and chew out that old priest. He was going to write a letter to the bishop and ask why the church allowed pedophiles but not a marriage between two people who deeply love each other. By the time we went to Easter mass the subject was still on her mind, but she quietly took a step toward liberation on her own.

I refuse to have my previous marriage annulled by paying a couple thousand dollars and going before a tribunal. How can deep pockets get me into heaven? My soul belongs to me. Spiritual matters that involve paying off a church are the ultimate hypocrisy. Christ chased the moneychangers out of the temple, but a few of them remain behind. Diana still dreams of a Catholic wedding in a church. Of all my wishes for her I don't have an answer to this predicament. I had to have a hands-off approach because I know Diana has to arrive at her own conclusions. Denis and Carol spoke in my behalf. Easter diner was celebrated with an opening prayer. I failed to grow any horns.

Our time in Ireland came to a close with warm goodbyes and a promise to return. My calls to Denis and Carol are always interrupted by a request to speak directly to Diana. To have her loved and accepted by my best friend is a true gift. She passed the test. She has passed every test.

Chapter 10. Costa Rican Journal

We have been in Costa Rica for exactly two weeks and I've just turned on the computer for the second time. The first time was to upload some photographs from my camera. It's been in the back of my mind, just like my intent to study Spanish every day. Well not so fast. I've become a homeowner and the priorities of working on the house are top shelf.

The day we arrived we took a taxi to Alujuaia to make the payment for the condo maintenance to Oscar, the man I bought my condo from. The monthly maintenance rate went up about eighteen dollars a month because of a new drinking water system. I am lucky in that the man I bought my condo from is also the associations treasurer. He keeps the books. I make sure I pay in advance. His business is five minutes from the airport, so usually I make a stop at his business and then take the bus to Jaco afterwards. This time, because Diana was never here before we took a van, we didn't reserve our bus tickets, which could mean standing for three hours on the bus. The price difference is seventeen dollars each. The bus is $3.50. We had four huge bags so I wanted to make this as easy on Diana as possible.

We got into Jaco Beach around six o'clock and didn't do much but look at the problems with the house and go to bed. I noticed that water had come from the ceiling into the back room and warped the furniture, causing terrible mold smells in the small room we always sleep in. We moved into a larger room the next few nights until we discarded the mattress. We thought we could salvage it, which was a three-day process of spraying bleach and leaving it in the sun. But in the end we decided the smell was too strong and the whole box spring set was given to the head security guard, Eric. We also gave him a TV that was on the blink. The TV worked fine the last time, but sat unused for a year. Hopefully it will still be saved with a small repair bill. Eric was happy to have these things even though we told him of the potential problems. As it turned out the roof was leaking because the neighboring condo had built a new roof over their patio. They did not correctly seal the wall. No flashing was used. A three-inch gap permitted the water to flood my place. Eric climbed on the roof with me where we discovered the opening. Who ever they hired to do this work should have been aware enough to see a problem was in the making.

We unpacked the second day and consolidated the four bags down to two. The rest of the luggage is for Diana's family in Colombia. We are Santa Claus when ever we go back to Colombia. This is an area I tug at Diana about. She feels so obliged to bring gifts. I feel like the best gift is our return and the time we will spend with them. But I admit I get into the gift buying and have added my share of the load to the luggage. I know we will return with one bag, and that will grow to two if we do the expected buying in Panama.

I can't begin to recall the number of projects I have done in the past few weeks. Last night, after building a door out of tongue and grove lumber, I begged Diana to make me stop working. The door took three days to build. I can go and go, and keep running like that friggen pink rabbit on TV; my batteries never run out. The ideas keep coming. At night I lay in bed thinking of what to do next and how to solve problems in the house. I fixed the roof leak by getting on top of the house and adding some improvised aluminum gutters. Eric had a few strips of aluminum and I asked him for them. After my labors a tremendous down pour occurred. My work was a success. I was in the room watching for water, nothing but smiles. The water was coming down in buckets outside and my first major problem was solved.

A couple of days later we had the old wooden windows in the front of the condo replaced with new aluminum windows. That was a whole day cleaning and picking up as the workers made a mess. Jason, a Canadian who lives here in the complex helped me arrange to buy the windows. I had second thoughts about doing the windows because they were so expensive. The workers showed up the day before, demanding we pay because the materials had already been cut. This turned out to be a lie. I saw the glass was uncut when they arrived the next morning. Nothing was hurt, but it caused a small wrinkle in my relationship with Jason. He had spent the energy to get them here to do a bid before our arrival. As it turned out the old windows were full of ants and the wood was pretty rotten from the humid weather. The new windows allow much more air to flow though the house, which was my main concern.

Of course the windows being installed caused the door-frame to shift and we had a bit of a scare when the lock jammed. We were stuck outside; I was cursing because I didn't think to try the lock before we shut the door to go to the market. I borrowed a screwdriver from Jason's wife Milagros and several hours later we were back in business and safe inside. I had to grind down the door parts to insure they worked. One thing leads to another. The windows are dark and the louvers allow a good amount of air in. The cross ventilation is very poor so I have hanging fans in the windows. This is my alternative to air-conditioning, which is very costly here. I also don't like what it does to my sinuses.

As I began to write this tonight Diana was in the back room doing a jazzercise video. She started her new routine and I figured it was time to get into the writing. It was a way to excuse myself from exercising with a video tape, something I've always hated to do. I'll swim and workout on a treadmill but to stand and dance is not something I've been able to do.

Before we left for Costa Rica I had a vision of walking on the beach every morning and reciting Spanish as we got some exercise. Instead I did lose weight, but I sweat it out by working my butt off in the house. I've ridden my bicycle to the hardware store so many times that I lost a few pounds doing that. I was talking with Diana on our way back from the beach today, "Is it me, or is the weather cooler this week?" We think so. The first week we both sweat like mad. The nights were even grueling. The first few days our bodies adjusted to the humidity and heat. I know at night, if I leave the fan running, I wake up feeling like a puffed up fish, but I feel worse if I sleep in the air conditioning.

Saturday we rented a motorcycle for twenty-four hours. We used the time to ride up to a waterfall about twenty miles away. We rode up the mountain and walked down into a valley, just as far and steep as the other. At the entrance ($15 each, yikes) the man told us that we would be forty minutes down and forty-five back. How stupid we were to believe that lie! It took us an hour to get down, and I mean get down. The decline was a workout. My shirt was soaking wet by the time we arrived at the swimming "hole". It was more like a knee-deep bath. No one else was around as we stripped and put on our bathing suits, ate lunch (shit cakes), and cooled down to a reasonable heart rate. Shit cake is the unique invention of Diana. The day before she improvised a casserole that came out of the oven looking like burnt shit. We had a great laugh looking at the concoction and I gave it the appropriate name. At first my label for her cooking hurt her, but she laughed harder than I did. It was an anniversary surprise she had made the day before. I refuse to waist food, so we put it in a left over container and brought it along with oranges and frozen bottles of water. We also had some strange baked cheese sticks that are a Costa Rican favorite I have seen people eating on the bus rides. The food turned out to be very tasty. We sat next to the river and looked at the sun high above the rain forest. The sound of the river filled our ears, but the sound of birds somewhere off in the distance would periodically pierce the roaring waters. We had a beautiful relaxing afternoon next to the running river.

I never did see the waterfall we paid so dearly descending into the steamy, hot valley to see. Diana did, but only because she left for the top a few minutes before me. I was putting on my shoes and told her to go ahead. Diana took a wrong turn not fifty meters from the swimming hole, and sauntered up to see the waterfall. By the time I finished putting on my shoes and entered the trail I was ahead of her, not knowing so, and asking a group of German tourists if they had seen my wife. They hadn't and I was sure she was lost, which she was. To get lost on a trail that goes a direction you've just come from is beyond me. The whole thing lasted long enough for Diana to tell me she was screaming and having a panic attack. But she did see the falls! "Did you at least take a picture?" "No, I was too scared." As long as it took me to tie my shoe laces and put on my back pack, my new wife of one year nearly vanished into her own fear.

We retraced our path and reached the top. This took some two hours after we began our "forty-five minute" walk back to the top. When I got to the top, the gatekeeper asked me where my wife was in Spanish. In Spanish I answered, "dead". We both got a good laugh because he and I both knew she was struggling up that path nearing exhaustion.

At the entrance we bought a large bottle of water and poured it into the last remaining tube of ice in our plastic bottles.

Ice water! The second man working at the entrance helped us repair the foot rest on the rented motorcycle. We sat and talked for a few more minutes. The Costa Rican people are very easy to be with and make small talk. We rode down the mountain with a bit of anticipation because the break peddle was so bent. My foot barely fit on the bracket. But I skillfully maneuvered over each bump until we made our way to the main highway.

When there I made a right turn, a direction we had not come from, and we headed toward the river to see a family of crocodiles. The ride was much smoother on the highway, but large trucks and buses gave us a small push as they'd pass. Fifteen minutes later we reached the rivers bridge. In all we counted sixteen crocodiles in various sizes and shapes. Diana said it was the first time she had seen a crock outside of a zoo. The bridge over the river gives a birds-eye view of a group of smiling crocodiles that would gobble us up in a minute had we not the safety of the bridge above. I think they just sit there and mock all the tourist spectators who come to gasp. I'm certain they sit and watch with aching bellies, well aware that some day, some how, some one is going to lean just an inch too far and a banquet shall begin. I don't know how they get so large, but I suspect the cattle ranchers nearby miss a head now and then.

Our anniversary started out terrible. I was rude and short with Diana about being so slow. I gave my, "Why are you so blah, blah, blah." speech. By the afternoon I'm sure she had enough and was thinking of divorce, something any romantic feels when the grind of the relationship pulls them down. I think I was just fed up with being with Diana non-stop for almost eleven days. No matter how much I love my wife there are times I need time alone, but that hadn't been the case. The day before she finally got sick of my complaints enough to go to the Internet cafe and call her cousin in Florida. I wish I could have been the listening fly on the wall. (Would that make me a Spanish fly?) It took us half the day to become friends again. I gladly admit we pulled it off. I lay the surprise anniversary gifts out on the bed; a Costa Rican blouse and a nice necklace made of precious stones. I had bought them the day before under the guise of a hardware store run. I actually did go to the hardware store, but I had to wait an hour for the tiny shop to open so I could buy the necklace.

We got dressed up. Diana wore a pretty dress we bought in New York City on one of our failed conciliate visits. It was raining so we took a taxi to the end of town and shared a plate of shrimp and a plate of ceviche. We bought more gifts for the family in a small shop and had a dessert in another shop that was indescribable. It was a Chi-tea smoothie with cinnamon and a spice that I've never tasted before. I have no idea what it was, but we've been back twice already to enjoy this cold drink. We ended the night quite successfully with a little wine and romance. I don't even want to know the name of the spice drink just to keep the magic of our anniversary. Not everything good should be known and clearly defined. I've managed to stay uncritical for three days now. A good thing.

That goes for a good relationship as well. We humans spend more time defining what the problems are than looking at the beauty of something that works well. We remember the infractions more than we recall special tender moments. In our relationship there are many complex dimensions at work. What I as a North American sluff-off as personality differences Diana sees as huge cultural differences. "In my culture…" is a flash point for me to begin thinking "here it comes". I think part of this is my American psyche, which is a kind of A-cultural, "what's the big deal about", society. We see ourselves as Americans first, then comes the root countries identity. We melt our cultures and homogenize them into one. There is also the "immigrant mentality", which Lilia, the Unitarian minister that married us pointed out. In my dark heart I think it's just an excuse to hide behind the banner of culture, and to remain unchanged and complacent.

But despite my view Diana sees her country and cultural identity as a big reason that motivates her behavior. She refers to America as a "machine". A label/title I agree with but have little control over as a whole. God knows I hated the machine and fought against it in my own way for many years. One of my biggest attacks on my father was to call him a "robot" and rant about the "System". The System isn't pretty to the new immigrant 'kid on the block", but the system has now given me the luxury of affording a wife that is an economic project, and a life where travel is crucial to my mental survival. I guess the best way to explain, or justify, my youthful rebelliousness with my current middle class status is that I did it my way. I didn't buy into the System until I was in my forties. I can continue the revolution when I teach and empower others. Of course no matter how cool I think I am, the young find me old and see me through the eyes of unforgiving, youthful criticism. Coming to a third world country where the air is cleaner, the small vegetables and fruit have spots, and the hype of "sophistication" hasn't spoiled the people, is all part of my continued rejection of my own roots. My job as an educator gets balanced out by the time I recharge my batteries while away. So I am in a "catch-22" with my younger wife. I spent my time in the starving-artist trenches and fought against the machine. Now I just want to enjoy the fruits of my labors. There are many things I don't like about my country. Being an American doesn't make me an automatic proponent of the system.

Second Entry: A dragonfly balanced on barbwire. That was what I saw today on my way to the hardware store. I ride through paved streets that are completely vacant of houses and people. It is just a few minutes from my condo. It's like a ride in the country. As I ride I look at tiny birds that sit perched on the tall grasses singing beautiful melodies. These vacant lots will be full of condos in a matter of years, but for now I can pretend it will be this way forever. The bulk of my day was again repairing, replacing, and not resting. The main sewer pipe plugged up and I literally dug poop out of the pipe. That was before we went of to the hardware store.

My video camera is broken, no juice, and that is a major issue. It worked fine the day we rented the motorcycle. We brought it home in a backpack, set it on the bed, and a few hours later, nothing. It may be from moisture in the backpack or the bumpy ride on the motorcycle. I brought my friend Jose the same camera type a couple of years ago, so we have been exchanging batteries to test the camera, but nothing worked. It is on its way to the repair shop today. That may take a couple of weeks. Jose has loaned me his camera in the mean time.

I got miffed at Diana yesterday morning about buying all this food, which set the wrong tone for the day. I sat down and said, as "non-ugly" as possible that the money and food needed to be conserved. A Colombian woman we met at a Colombian restaurant (the only one in Jaco) has a door to door (out of her car) business selling Colombian foods. Before the woman came I talked to Diana that we needed only get a few things because we will be gone for a three day trip. Thirty dollars later, and much more than we could possibly eat. I was pissed.

The hardest part of the relationship is trying to maintain my own sense of self-control and balancing it with my partner's habits. The food is a big issue because I put on weight very easily. I also like to control my food intake by the amount of food I buy. There are times I've actually got angry when a huge plate, that Diana lovingly cooked, is put down in front of me. "I don't want to get fat by eating all this food." So when Diana bought the food I was feeling like excess was at play. She said much of the food was a gift for the people who we are about to go visit, but I've watched the way she spends money. I have a system in place for myself that allows for treats, but I never buy things that are fattening and bring them into the house.

Keeping the balance of having a close interpersonal relationship, and maintaining my own life style, is a big challenge. Diana moves through time and space at a much slower pace. When we walk or ride the bicycles I am constantly stopping and turning around to see where she is. No mater how slow I go she is behind and I feel like I'm waiting. Something I hate to do. Some of this is the physical smallness of her body size, but much of it is in an attitude of pace. She is very non aggressive, and in some ways not time oriented in the same way as I. When I go somewhere, I get there as fast as I can. Even on vacation I feel driven, directed, and purposeful.

One day (the angriest I've become) we were going to the Colombian restaurant to buy arepas (a Colombian flat bread made of corn). I crossed the street and rode about one block. Diana had crossed the street and walked the entire way to where I was. She stopped several people asking them where the restaurant was (which I already knew), and walked her bike. This set me off and I proceeded to yell at her, which is something I've never done in public. This time I was livid. I find this beyond understanding. How can you make a person wait and why walk a bike when it has wheels? These are small things that add up to big ones. The New Yorker and the Colombian have pacing issues, which is no surprise.

Travel Entry: In the complex where I own my condo we met a Costa Rican couple named Jose and Sandra. Over a period of several days we socialized with them and the Canadian who also lives in the complex. Jose is a farmer who has done very well for himself. Sandra is a stay at home mom who raised two sons. We enjoyed each others company so much that they invited us to their home in a town south-east of San Jose, the Capitol. The town is Cartago. Because of many common cultural traits such as the language, their religious beliefs, and the foods, Diana felt especially at home with our new friends. It is always very refreshing to make new friends. At this point in our vacation it was time to give us some space and get away from the projects in the house.

We took the bus into San Jose's main bus terminal and switched buses for Cartago. Three and a half hours from our departure we arrived and Sandra was waiting at the bus stop with her son, Fabio. He is a tall young man of twenty fours years. Unlike most Costa Ricans he is big boned and has a large body frame, yet he is as gentle as a lamb. He spoke some English, so he and I would venture into side conversation while the rest of the family spoke Spanish with Diana.

Their house was a small palace. We drove up and I was immediately surprised by the size of the building. I joked with Jose asking him where the cows were. I did expect a little finca with fences and cows grazing. The house was in a suburban neighborhood. I need to explain that suburban in Costa Rica isn't like in the USA. A dilapidated shack could be next to a modern house. The streets have pits and patched holes. No newly paved street has ever been left alone, in a matter of weeks a gas line or some kind of construction reverts any new pavement to a lumpy surface.

The front of the house had a large garage door that opened into a grand entrance door. The minute we entered the house we were in a well kept and luxurious environment. Two big white sofas were situated between matching stuffed chairs. The floor was white marble. A long dinning room table with freshly cut flowers (grown by Sandra) was behind the sitting area. We were escorted to the master bedroom and told to put our bags in there. In the back of the house was a large kitchen where a house keeper was making dinner. We were given a tour of the upstairs where a curved glass window had a view of the nearby city center. In the back of the house an orchid greenhouse was in full bloom. Sandra's pride was her green thumb for growing orchids. Fabio had two small puppies in a pin and showed us the yard behind the house. There a gigantic boulder stood out. He noted this was his major playground when growing up. Down a steep slop was a rocky river with more large boulders. The front of the house looked like a massive garage door, the rest was a wonder of spacious marble rooms.

We gave them the Colombian foods and sat down to eat and have long conversation. I'd speak in broken Spanish and Fabio, or Diana, would translate what I couldn't. I took an instant liking to Fabio. He was recently graduated from college and looking for a job, but with little success. He had been looking for six months. He had a girlfriend but she lived in San Jose and they saw each other on weekends when they could. I could see a very solid person and deep character in this young man. We felt at home and relaxed with our new friends.

Soon we all piled into the family SUV and had a brief tour of Cartago. Our first stop was a ruin of stone cathedral that had been devastated by an earthquake. This mammoth structure was over one hundred years old. All that remained were the solid thick walls and pieces of the ceiling that lay around like old dinosaur bones. Inside this roofless church was a garden and stone paths that ran the length of the yard in symmetrical directions. The church had been rebuilt more than once due to reoccurring earthquakes, yet no major earthquakes had occurred since the abandonment of the building. The doorways all had thick metal gates, which were locked, but a full view of the insides were possible.

Our second stop was to the most impressive human structure in all of Costa Rica, the Cathedral of Cartago. The building is gray and white, more or less a bland color scheme, but a colossal structure. On the inside there is a stark contrast to its exterior; colorful tile floors and a high ceiling of wood, painted in deep dark browns which replaced the drab grays of the exterior. After seeing the ceiling I came to realize the building was primarily built of wood. The style of the church seemed Byzantine because of the repeated arches and series of support columns that opened into a huge central dome. The alter had a tall gold tabernacle with a relic. Inside was a small relic called the Black Virgin.

The legend of the Black Virgin is based on a series of miracles where a young peasant girl finds a carved rock with an image of the Virgin holding the Christ child. The girl is in a river while washing her clothes. The young girl tells the local priest of her find and he wants to see this small (five inch) anomaly. The girl returns home only to find the stone has vanished. A few days later the girl is again washing in the river and finds the stone. Again she returns to the priest, this time with the stone. He locks the stone to keep it safe but the stone vanishes despite the lock and key. Again the girl finds the stone in the forest in the river. A miracle is declared and people begin to make pilgrimages to see the Virgin. The small river is a source of holy water that people use to cure disease and illnesses. Over the years thousands of tiny amulets have been left on the walls discarded by cured believers. These amulets are in the shapes of legs, hearts, arms, airplanes, boats, or any small remembrance where people declare the Black Virgin has saved their lives.

The Cathedral stands on the grounds where the relic was found and the tiny stream is now a series of water faucets where the believers collect the holy water. Around the back of the cathedral a museum displays the amulets and a diorama of the peasant girl praying to the Virgin. This church is by far the largest in Costa Rica, and the most articulate in design. We returned to Jose and Sandra's home for fruit drinks, pastries, and conversations around the dinner table in the kitchen.

The next morning we waited for Jose to return from his fields. He had already been out working since five in the morning. Jose had traveled and studies agriculture in many countries from Europe to Cuba. He showed us photographs of the early days when he was in a cooperative and he was very poor. He worked twelve hour days raising potatoes and onions. Eventually he began to buy his own small parcels of land and little by little created a decent wage. He and his family had vacationed in many countries and bought the condo in Jaco when it was first being built eighteen years earlier. After breakfast we climbed into the new SUV and headed up the mountain road to see his lands and wave at the field workers as we passed. He'd wave at the locals in trucks or in the fields like any Nebraska farmer. Everyone knows everyone else.

The road was well paved and wound up the mountain like a snake. Eventually we began to see the valley far below and another range of mountains on the far side of Cartago. The views were breath taking. As we climbed the air became increasingly thin and crisp. Green lush vegetation rolled over the hills like honey. The humidity of the valley was replaced by cold dry air that smelled of flowers and green, green, green colors. We were no longer in Costa Rica, or rather the low lands of the tropical beaches I had been so familiar with. We rose higher and higher each turn exposing a lush green terrain of new and different foliage. The ecosystem was drastically becoming canvases with broad leaf plants and tiny flowering bushes. We were above the clouds. White puffy drifts of clouds would pass over the road as we drove to our destination, the Irazu Volcano.

We paid a small entrance fee and parked the car after going further into a sanctuary. There were maybe three other cars in the parking lot. We walked down a long path with nothing but gray volcanic dust, occasionally seeing plants with strange tall chutes and gigantic broad leafs. The opening was as large as four soccer fields. The top of the mountain had been blown away in the sixties, the same day President Kennedy visited Costa Rica. As we walked half a mile or so, to the right was a crater where a lake once lay. We approached a wooden fence not much further beyond where a crater, at least an eighth of a mile below, looked like a giant spoon had scooped out the earth. At the bottom lay a green lake with sulfur gases bubbling up to the surface. It looked like a witches brew where the heat and fumes kept the stark terrain lifeless. Along the rims of the crater green plants ringed the edge. Above a cloudless sky exposed bright blue heavens, but the horizon was filled with rolling white cumulus clouds. Spaced openings in the clouds allowed us to see the mountains below. Jose pointed out another nearby volcano, but all I saw was a faint green indication of land far below.

After being in a fascinating lunar landscape and alien garden, we descended half way down the mountain to a volcano museum with a small café. The café had a string of hummingbird feeders with the buzzing chaotic traffic of dozens of iridescent hummingbirds. I took out the zoom lens for a rare close encounter with these tiny wondrous creatures. At the table we had hot coco and cookies. While I was sitting I looked at Fabio's hands. He had a rare birth defect where his perfectly shaped hands are missing one finger. He took the question in stride and answered that he was a highly evolved human being.

We continued further down into the valley passing Jose's farm, eventually passing through the town of Cartago to the opposite side of the range. Here we entered more rough tropical terrain and an entirely different type of land lay ahead of us. We parked the car at a public park and walked to the edge of a grand valley. A small town was visible a mile below where we stood. The afternoon sky was dark in some places as a passing rain shower spread a long strand of water like lace over the green forest. We were in a much hotter environment in a matter of an hours drive, from outer space to the jungles. In the park families sat at concrete tables and ate lunch or played catch with Frisbees. I remembered such intimate family outings in California when I was young.

We soon were in the same town we had seen from the high park. We headed toward the opposite end where a series of small bridges put us over rapid, rocky creeks with boulders half the size of the SUV. The road was increasingly broken down. Deep groves made the ride bumpy as Jose maneuvered the car in a skillful dance between the ridges. We reached a long single-lane bridge. Fabio and I walked across to make sure it was safe, then signaled Jose to proceed. On the opposite side we gathered for a look at the river. Jose explained that we were at the edge of one of Costa Rica's largest National Parks. We hadn't seen a village for a quarter of an hour and it felt like we reached the end of civilization. We retraced a portion of the travel and cut across the river to a new road and an increasingly populated area. Here large plantations of tropical plants, used for fruit drinks, had massive nets to keep out birds that ate the fruits. This side of the river was not rustic, but well paved and much faster to travel on. Field workers with tall black rubber boots and long machetes were walking home after a days work. The grime on their clothes and exhausted look on their brows added to the slow pace as they sauntered on the roads side. As we approached they made an effortless side step to get out of the way of our vehicle. It was getting late and we all wanted to eat. We found a town and pulled into a restaurant with an armed guard standing out front holding a sleek black rifle. This is a sign that the restaurant is popular. The restaurant had large TV's hanging in various places where a soccer game was being broadcast. We ignored the TV's, ate, and continued our visit. The same armed security guard that welcomed us pulled out three umbrellas and escorted us to the car as a typical afternoon rain shower passed, causing steam to rise off the hot black asphalt. The dusty road was now beginning to clear.

In the evening we sat around and talked at length. A power outage, common in Costa Rica, brought out the candles as we laughed at the joy of such a nice inconvenience. In the morning Jose was long at his labors in the field when Fabio and Sandra took us back to the bus stop. The line into the bus was on a sidewalk. As soon as a bus left a new line of people was already waiting to board the next bus. It was the morning rush hour. A man begging for money sat on a wall exposing his open wounds as flies buzzed on and off of his sick leg. No one was shocked, but many people gave him a small coin to help. Some people gave him bottled water and portions of their lunch. We rode the bus back to San Jose and then the last leg of our journey to Jaco Beach.

Third Entry: Yesterday Diana and I ran into a Colombian man I used to hang out with at the condominiums. His name is Carlos. We spent a few hours here and there in town, sitting and exchanging stories. His English is weak and we both were teaching each other our languages. Diana and I ran into him at the little Colombian restaurant we go to buy Colombian arepas. In conversation Carlos asked me how my daughter was. I said he was mistaken. I have no daughter. Then I made a joke like, oh that's a secret don't talk about that. Diana got angry and was quiet about it. Fast forward to making love this morning and Diana comes out with the question "You promise not to put on the ugly?" (This is the phrase that I know will follow by some question that she is really feeling doubts and lack self esteem. Ninety percent of the time it is a question directed at me, my past, or my motives.) We were still making love, and the question came up. But I know the problem is looming. I asked her to wait with the question until later.

We finished with our activity and I began the inquiry as to the question that she was afraid to ask. Only I knew it's going to be about the daughter that I never had. Of course the dance takes many steps to get to the real issue. By this time I'm already angry but really trying to keep my cool. I have been repeatedly asked why I married her, if I married her just to have sex, and now this next question. All these questions imply to me that I'm some kind of liar who is trying (or did deceive her). So I get angry just at her innuendo. I didn't put on the ugly. I was direct and didn't try to nurse her self-doubt and self-pity. This is how I see all these questions.

Long story short, she is off walking at the beach, and sulking because I'm some kind of monster. I told her she needed some psychological counseling because she is the one creating problems on a beautiful morning in a beautiful place, when there are none. I resent being questioned and I resent the directives when she left, telling me where to clean and what to do. All this concerns me. It's very difficult to maintain independence when a person is very dependent, and that person is insecure.

The other day the questions were about sharing the bed I slept in with another woman. It was a friendship where we never had sex and the woman had her baby between us. The house was full of people and there were no extra beds. This is nothing new about my past. I've been, perhaps, too open to share the stories, but they surely aren't meant to create what is happening with the "doubting Dennis game". I reject her for these reasons. I want her to grow up and get beyond this line of questioning. I lost it and screamed at her about the bed incident.

I was reading a passage by Khrisnamurti yesterday. The idea was to put my ego aside, that no one can really harm us, that the ego and our self-image get offended because we forget that we are not our bodies. Then I was wondering if Khrisnamurti ever had a wife tapping him on the chest and invading his personal space. I'll tell Diana that she is in my space, and she reacts by asking me questions precluded by, "Do you mind if I ask you a question". Or, "I don't want to invade your space but...". So this extreme reaction only exacerbates the issue and I get really tired of the game. It's all a great test of my patience. Because of the language barrier I am constantly translating what Diana really means. Her English is very weak and I have to filter through the true meaning. In the middle of a heated exchange I have to stop and clarify her English. That is the first obstacle, and then comes the psychological angle of what is behind the intent.

Diana has two sides. One is weak and needy. The other is a happy child. She even has a different tone of voice. That is the side of her that is most pleasant to be around because she is fun and nice to be around. The other side is an unfinished problem in motion. I know for myself I've reached a point in my life where I'm not into being depressed, or heavy. I have a Zen approach. My modes are pretty stable. It is a true test to be around another person for a length of time under any circumstance. Diana is beautiful around other people and at her best in social situations. Yet I can get a lecture afterwards as to, how in her culture it is correct to.... blah, blah, blah. My response is did I offend anyone? I'm fifty-five years old and I've been successfully interacting with people for all these years. Now I need a coach! Please!!! These are the challenges to marrying a person from a foreign country whom is younger and less experienced. But she is wonderful to be around most of the time, or I'd be bonkers. I'll cope.

Fourth Entry: It is around five in the morning, there is thunder in the distance, the birds are beginning to sing and the mountains near by have a glow of light that indicates sunrise in another half hour, or so. Yesterday was full of events that add up to a chain of people and circumstance that weave a story almost too complicated, and too boring to be history, but just the simple day to day life here. Our day started with Johnny not showing up at eight. He is the teenager I met one day while trying to take Diana her bicycle to the church. Diana was already there and I needed to bring her bicycle. A young man was walking and I asked him where he was going. He obliged and rode her bicycle to church. I was riding my bike and have seen the way people guide a second bike along side. I almost crashed many times, but Johnny was there a short while after I began.

Anyway, Johnny and I met and he helped me solve a problem. A couple of days later I was going to the beach with Diana and we saw Johnny where he lives. A few days later I went looking for him and found him. I asked him if he would help me paint and work on the concrete walls. We shook hands and made a deal for eight hundred Colons an hour. (About a dollar twenty-five an hour) I asked how much he charged and let the price be set by him. He was to show up at seven in the morning. He worked for two days and made about fifteen dollars each day. He showed up ten minutes late every day.

The third day he didn't show after asking the previous day if he could come an hour later. We agreed. At twelve thirty he came to work, by the time we had finished much of the cleaning. Diana sent him away. Johnny didn't make eye contact with me, but I could see he wasn't happy to lose the work. I have a thing about being on time and don't second-guess an opportunity. Diana and I had conversation all day, before and after he was here. It was about responsibilities and where they truly lay. I paid him a little above the standard wage here. He lives in poverty with his child and girlfriend. What more can I do to help him?

Diana hired a girl last week to help clean. The girl is a friend of Jose, my long time friend here. The girl showed up an hour and a half late. Diana paid her twenty dollars, four days worth of wages. I was furious because I felt Diana had been taken advantage of, but Diana saw it as a gift and generosity. I would never reward lateness and certainly not over pay. So it is a fine line between what is generosity and what is really an honest exchange. Do we always need to teach? Are we to teach loving kindness or teach responsibility? If I were Johnny I'd be five minutes early and if I couldn't make it, due to illness like he said, I'd go let the people know. So I believe Johnny is making his own bed and nothing I can do will change him and his situation. Do we negatively enable or do we empower others? That is the question.

We came to find out that Johnny has a twenty five day old child and a girlfriend that is nineteen like him. I saw him on a Moped a few hours later while going to the grocery store. He smiled and I returned a smile, but that was it. I wonder, as an educator, if stating the obvious is really needed. I think in some ways we should have told him that he was late and lost the job because of that. Instead Diana told him we did the work already, but we hired another woman to do the cleaning. Johnny's reason for not coming in the morning was that he had a stomach ache. I don't believe him.

We did a lot of cleaning and I did some touchup painting on a few things. I organized the patio where I had built an extra storage space a year ago. When I did the roof repair this year I unwittingly created a nice living space for an animal. Which was a fear that came true last night. The sheet of aluminum on the eves of the house made a great apartment for a large sized creature. I thought an iguana would take up residency but last night the sound of plastic rustling sent me out with the camera to capture a photo of a possum. He was going though the plastic bags. I had organized my things in plastic bags up in the storage area. Now today I have a new project to begin, a metal screen to keep intruding animals from my patio. Diana wouldn't come to bed last night because she was afraid of the animal coming into the open door. I have a lace curtain that acts as a screen door. First light this morning I was up on the ladder seeing if my friend was still in the long dark apartment. My light wasn't good enough so I'll know more later.

Carlos came by at four, as we had planned, and we ate an early dinner. He is the man that thought I had a daughter. The subject didn't come up. Carlos is from Medellin, like Diana. He works here and sends the money to his wife and two children. He works as a welder. When I met him a couple of years ago he was working in a hotel, and a second job in a restaurant. Now his life is much better. He shared one of the condos a couple of door down with two other men. When I saw him the other day I, embarrassingly, didn't remember his name and mistook him for the man who replaced our windows. He took it well. Last year he would stop by my house and we'd learn each other's language.

I'm about to make a breakfast of cereal, raw bran, bananas, and fruit yogurt drink. Yum, yum. The sun just popped over the horizon into the house. It's going to be a brilliant day.

It started to rain shortly after I wrote the entry today, that was a couple of hours ago. I just returned form speaking with my friend Jose. He is very close to me. We both have this love for talking about the internal life we all live. A kind of spiritual, twelve steps, recovery, quasi-enlightenment, that I assume most artists, or creative types have. But really the door to such states isn't exclusive to anyone. The kingdom of God is within us all.

The longest and best friend I have had in Costa Rica is Jose. Not the farmer, Jose is a surfer. I have known him for eight years. On all my trips to Costa Rica our path has crossed. Over the years our friendship has deepened. Jose talks about his relationship with the mother of his second child. They were married here in Costa Rica. It ended about a year ago. She is a "Gringa" from Utah. We talk about how important it is to know about the impatience we have with others, it is really impatience with ourselves. Blaming others is such a mind trap. How do I learn to express simple needs (like healthy cooking for instance), in a constructive way to my wife verses an intolerant demand? My relationship with my wife is there for a reason and purpose. All the conflict is there for a reason. We enter relationships knowingly or unknowingly with emotional ties that fill some kind of need. In my heart I want enough time to pass that the relationship becomes solid. My fear is that my destructive, impatient side will over-ride that period of growth. It is not easy to be married, but I prefer this state of commitment verses the way I dealt with "instant escape" when I was younger. Two failed marriages is nothing to be proud of. Yet, this time I have a lot more self-esteem and awareness. I have matured.

Ultimately we can only be responsible for ourselves. The real power in a healthy relationship comes from giving to and serving our partner. The same goes with life in general. Since I've been teaching, I gained much for myself by giving. I laugh at people who think teachers have it easy. Nothing can be more challenging than dealing with immature people. A test of my self-will is in constant motion. Yet it is a hit and miss game. Some people are reached by instruction, some are never reached, and the rest are in process of getting there. But right now, I have the luxury of not even thinking about the classroom. I love my conversations with Jose because they are all about self reflection, something we both do.

Fifth Entry: We leave in five days. Yesterday we bought the bus tickets. It's three dollars fifty cents for both of us to get to Alajuela and the airport. We have to be in the airport at 6:30AM, so we are going in the day before, rather than feel stressed about getting there on time. The hotel is five minutes from the airport. The public bus and hotel will be about the same as the expensive van for foreigners. The bus company has a new computerized system. The lines are shorter and the tickets can now be bought far in advance. In the twelve years since I first came here, the country is modernizing. Jaco is growing in leaps and bounds.

Yesterday it rained almost the entire day. I had a deep nap that was like being in heaven. Diana would come in and give me "boletas" (small face massages in round circles). We went to buy the bus ticket and Jose came by at three thirty as planned. We all went to Bejuco, which is the beach where Jose has bought some property. His place is about a half mile from the beach. It is a piece of land at this point.

We went in Julio's father's car. Julio is a young friend of Jose who is in the same twelve step program (so much for their anonymity). There was another man with them who had a prosthesis. The man is in his seventies. Apparently he feel asleep, drunk, on the railroad tracks and lost is right leg below the knee. He has been sober for a month now, the leg happened many years ago. I started a painting of the old man. His face is full of stories and pain.

We got back to Jaco after sunset and sat together and watched TV. A steam pipe blew up in New York City and we watched the mayor answering reporters until the whole thing was overkill. I think we went to bed around eight.

This morning we got up and went swimming in the ocean. I caught some good waves while body surfing. I wonder if I'm aging because I feel that my energy is now lower while I'm in the ocean. We've both lost a lot of weight (happily) while working in this heat. I was working out in New York. I went swimming, specifically, to be in better shape when I arrived here in the ocean. The first night I went out swimming I became exhausted and frightened from the tide. That first ocean encounter gave me a bit of fear to swim.

On the way to the beach we stopped and woke up Johnny. Diana did the talking. She said he had another opportunity to work with us, but he had to be on time. He said he knew she was serious. I shook his hand to secure the deal. Tomorrow we will have him repair a wall in the patio. I'll have him do some painting there also. Johnny gets a second chance and this time he knows he can't be late.

Today the sky is clear. All I've done is go to get money at the ATM and buy some wire fencing to keep the possum out of the eves of the house at night. Although last night the possum was nowhere to be seen. Diana doesn't want him back.

Diana and I have been on a good wavelength the last couple of days. I know how explosive I get and don't know really how to improve my behavior at those exact moments. We talk about this. I know I have to be a better husband. I justify my "badness" by explaining my progress. The frustration that pours out of me from time to time is like an eruption. Diana wants me to handle her with love and care, but my male hormones come out like a volcano erupting. Destructive behavior is counter-productive, yet I can't seem to contain the pressure. A few minutes later I'm fine, I got it out, but Diana suffers for the day when I explode.

All this internal frustration also comes out of me during sex and it is terrible for her. The angry occurrences are fewer and far between. I remember containing myself on the honeymoon, but feeling volatile. I think we are just getting to know each other and my abrupt moods will become fewer when we truly understand our sexual interaction. I've had more than a few sexual experiences and she has had very few, so the combination includes a lot of learning time. The ironic twist is the older man who wants the young virgin. The gap of experience creates a need to learn about each other. Each person is different and has a set of different needs and expectations. I would suggest to others to leave most of those experiences at the door when entering a new relationship because the whole process begins a new. Yes, maturity is a beautiful tool in handling what life and relationships bring. I am still learning. The important thing is to not be too "wise", or it will all come around and bite one in the butt.

Last Entry; July 24, 2007. We are about to leave. The house is very clean and I feel well with all the projects completed. We have a half hour in the airport. My biggest fear is coming to the airport on the wrong day, silly me. We took the bus yesterday because the plane leaves at 8:30 and the bus from Jaco had a departure time of 4 A.M., that would put us a half hour late for the two hour limit before the flight to be in the airport. The bus ride was nice because a rain shower made the weather pleasant. We said all our goodbyes to everyone in the compound, including the all-important security guards. The instructions were to allow no one in except for Oscar, the man I bought the house from.

We got to Alajuela around three thirty; found a hotel with the taxi driver. It was forty-five dollars for the night. We went to another hotel first where I've stayed before. They wanted seventy dollars. The new hotel was larger, just as good and it had big rooms. I had a very hot shower, and the people were nice too. The only problem was the room was on the third floor, but the taxi driver helped me take the bags up.

About three days before we left Jaco, Diana and I went to my favorite little cove. I was sad and astonished to see the gigantic tree I've sat under for twelve years was gone. The morning before we went for a swim in the same spot. We saw a bulldozer and I said something to the Gringo who was arriving, asking him what was up. He said a resort was being built. I said I've been coming there for twelve years and my "private beach" was about to change. I never envisioned them cutting all the trees and epically the huge shade tree. I was very sad. The tree was at least a couple hundred years old, was outside the parameter fence, and I never thought it would be gone. It wasn't just the one tree; it was dozens of palm trees as well. This kind of insanity makes me very upset.

Think of all the pleasure that tree gave to people coming to the little cove. I've painted the branches many times. In a flash it was destroyed. They can't close off the beach, but I'm afraid to see what comes next. The North American said a resort had bought the land. When I asked him if a road from the other side was coming he didn't answer, but that must be the case because the river kept the beach closed from traffic before. The death of a true friend. I guess this makes me a tree hugger, but I'm really sad at the destructiveness of investors who do this with no respect for nature. Oh sure, they will plant new trees and manicure the land, but that tree was doing no harm and adding nothing but beauty. This kind of "development" makes me ashamed of being an American.

The morning that we left we hired a woman to clean the house. Johnny never did come back to work so I did the project myself. While the cleaning was going on I made one more wooden shelf. I had started it the night before; painted the shelf and prepared the bracket for the wall. I did it in stages. It was a nice final project for the day. The cleaning woman left and I went for my last swim in the pool while Diana made some lunch. We ate like pigs the last few days to get rid of the excess food. We even brought a leftover container of rice and beans that we ate for dinner in the hotel room.

In Alajuela we walked the streets for about an hour, went to the traditional central market, and tried to find an Internet café. The town closes like a tomb at six. The rain was starting so we retreated to the hotel for the Democratic U-tube debate. We fly to Colombia through Panama in the morning.

Chapter 11. Colombian Journal Part 1.

First Entry: We have arrived in Colombia. It is our second day. The trip was uneventful with a two-hour stop in the Panama airport. Tuto, Diana's dad, was at the airport when we arrived. The airport is modern, the customs was a bit of a hassle because we had to stand in a long line and they went through our bags. We said we were in Costa Rica and the military police sent us to the inspection.

The other line went to the x-ray machine, which is a little faster. The process involves lifting each bag onto a conveyer belt and the military police search each bag. It's a harmless, invasive delay.

The highway into Medellin is a beautiful modern work. The highway comes off the high plane, where the airport is, onto a spectacular view of the city from on high. The graceful road curves downward into the city where the road suddenly ends and chaos instantly sets in. The first major road, in fact the first crossroad into the city, is an intersection with no traffic lights. It becomes a chancy endeavor. The traffic flows but who has the right of way is completely unclear. It may be better than a traffic light because the cars and trucks just keep flowing at a pace that out paces any obstructive time delays. We proceeded and in moments were back on a major highway again. The road disappeared at the crossroad and reappeared after we crossed a bridge.

The pollution is terrible and thick. Motorbikes are everywhere. The helmets and each rider have the license plate number in light-reflective letters on their helmets and mandatory vests. I like this idea. There are so many motorbikes that it is a great way of keeping the folks in compliance. Sometimes I noticed the second rider was wearing the wrong numbers, but hey, they had a reason. I'm more amazed that so many people had the correct license number on the vest and the helmet.

The taxi we were in almost slammed into the rear of another car but the driver had it together enough to save our lives. We put our three bags into the car and the last one went into the front seat as the three of us crammed our bodies into the small car. The driver wasn't happy with the cramped conditions. The rain on the wet street made the sliding halt stressful.

The city is more modern and the infrastructure is better than Costa Rica. Yet there is an instant sign of poverty and homelessness. The long tunnel into downtown Medellin has people camped out along the roads edge. This is their sanctuary, a place where no one will bother them and no one can sneak-up on them. They have their cardboard boxes and a few scraps of clothes, and enough air pollution to make one wonder how they can take it.

Occasionally I've seen a man changing his cloths or eating in this tunnel full of noise, dust, and speeding traffic. The city has great beauty, great poverty, and everything in between.

We pulled the luggage up five flights of stairs, ate a tasty lunch, and unpacked ourselves, and were into bed by eight o'clock. Diana's mom came home around five and instant tears flowed. Diana misses her family and city. These trips home are like the cement that holds her soul together. I can see how important the family is here. Life is rough and cracked like the streets and sidewalks, but inside the houses are clean and as modern as any place can be. The same goes with the importance of family here. There are so many people that the real anchor in ones life is the family.

I left my parents home in disgust when I was seventeen, so I know little about the super-bond that Diana has with her family. What I perceived as rebellious break from my family was really a healthy leap of faith from a dysfunctional group of screwed up people. My sanity came from running away from what I've come to learn is the only real support most people in the world treasure and need; family. I have a lot to learn about in this area. It amazes me how stable and civilized Diana's family is. They get perturbed at each other, but it's never at a crisis level like my family life was. They seem to know and accept life in a way that brings true contentment. Being content with just few material possessions, and more aware of each other's personal value is a gift I wish my countries people possessed.

Tuto's car is in the shop again and he just explained to me what the problem was, half of which I piece together with my limited Spanish. He doesn't know when the "white bullet" will be ready. The car is a twenty-seven year old white Fiat. He's had it painted white and rebuilt so many times that it is a work of art in the school of survival. I can attest with full certainly that the car does not comply with current air emission standards, Kyoto treaty or not. This car would be worth half the credits of China. But he loves it like a man with his horse from back in the old days.

INTERNET LOVE: HOW I MET MY WIFE

Today we went to the bank, withdrew cash, bought Diana some eyeglasses, and went to the grocery store. Diana was upset because the debit card that worked in Costa Rica didn't work here. We went to our favorite ice cream parlor that is akin to a 1950' soda shop in the States. The women all wear pretty little uniforms with hats and attend to you like you are royalty. There is something very comforting to me about that place. I feel like a little child going back in time, being treated to an ice cream Sunday is really special. I'm not worrying about my weight. I've gone down an entire pant size from working in the heat of Costa Rica. Tuto gave me a size 36 pair of blue jeans. They fit perfectly. I'm sitting writing in a little washroom with windows on two sides. I can see the city sprawling up on both sides of the valley and the evening lights are just being turned on. We are home again.

Second Entry: We went to a little town named La Ceja. The bus took about two hours and had frequent stops. It's about thirty miles over the ridge from Medellin. We arrived and went to sit in the town square. It was beautiful and a wonderful breeze was in the air. I took out a light jacket Tuto had loaned me. The mountains have a temperature difference of ten degrees from Medellin. Despite the fact that it's summer and we are not that far from the equator, it's chilly. In the town square I ate an avocado and crackers, something my mother taught me to love. I took photographs and we visited the church. Every town has the square, the park, and the church to look forward to seeing.

We walked a few blocks and asked two men where to eat cheap. They sent us in the right direction and we found the place in no time. The huge plate of rice, beans, yucca, potatoes, and a piece of chicken cost two dollars for both of us. I took more pictures and found some interesting subject matter in the bar, which was a collection of antique objects. I noticed the people didn't want their picture taken, I asked several of them.

We walked a few blocks and found ourselves on streets with no automobiles. The houses had people standing in the doorways. Diana stopped an old man and asked his permission for a photograph, he obliged. On the same street we saw a very interesting old man in a door and I asked to take his picture. He invited us into his house and gave me a tour of the family photographs on the wall. They had a collection of photographs from his fifty-year restating of the marriage vows. He had eight children. His son, an older man in his forties who had retardation, helped point out the shrine on the wall. They were especially proud of the electric light inside the shrine that illuminated the brass crucifix. I was clicking pictures the entire time. The man's wife was very quiet as she sat in a wheelchair. She was not in good shape. In the photos of their vows she was standing. I think a stroke put her in the chair. We said our goodbyes and continued on.

About a block further a man exited his house and got on his bicycle. He turned, saw us and got off the bike, and instantly invited us into his home. He explained he was helping a family who had been displaced by the guerillas. A second house next door was where he took us first. He asked where we were from and I said the United States. He wanted some one to see the conditions of this family. I wasn't sure if he wanted money or what, but we looked at the squalor and terrible condition of this very poor family. We later talked about this. Diana said he stated his needs, but didn't come right out and ask us for money. I video taped the encounter and took some photographs. The room where all the people slept had clothes laying everywhere and was in a filthy condition. The kitchen had one gas burner and looked nothing like a kitchen. The floors were dirt and the chaotic condition of the house was beyond belief.

The man led us into his back courtyard where he showed us the garden and a rather large yard. The children were working in the garden picking beans. In a short time he lead us into his house, which was nothing like the other house. This house was clean, had plants, paintings of clowns, and brass objects. We stepped into another dimension. We didn't give him any money, but I was feeling like reaching into my pockets. Of course I felt the sad weight of the poor "displaced" (as they are called in Spanish), but I was there as a visitor and observer.

We spent about seven minutes with this man and I was not sure how much longer we should be lingering because of our safety. We said our "thank you" and went out into the street again. As we walked towards a cemetery more men sat on street corners and one man followed us to the entrance of the cemetery. I asked him if I could take his picture, he refused, and I knew it was time to head back toward a safer, more populated, place. We both had an instinct to be where people were around, so we walked slowly back to the center of town. I can't really say we were in any kind of danger, but the poverty in the neighborhood didn't lend to a sight seeing atmosphere any more.

We bought a ticket to a faster bus home and were gone within minutes. I know Diana didn't like the day, she wanted to be around people and drinking coffee, but I think it was an adventure most people would never have tried. I've always had a lucky star of protection. We approach people and situations with a calm respect.

As we were lying in bed about to go to sleep Diana was saying how she didn't expect to be married to a "strange man". I don't get offended. She labels me as eccentric, but that isn't that bad. I asked her what she expected and she replied. She thought she would have children and a nice house. This is what happens when two people from two different countries link up. The house, American Dream, to me is a financial trap. I'd rather travel and see the world than be tied down to such a big responsibility. The children will come with time when Diana has her career and is more settled. If that doesn't happen it wasn't meant to be. Diana has a condition that seriously limits her ability to have children. I've long out lived my genetic and youthful ambitions to create a little mini-me. I want to plan and make sure I don't bare the full financial responsibility of a child. The blind leap of entering this marriage was enough to keep me satisfied. The unknown of a child is a huge leap. The challenge is clear to me. I never wanted to live like the "expectations" passed down from family and society. This was in my mind early on. Diana is coming from a totally different place. The middle is where we will continue to meet and create common ground.

Third Entry: We are at Diana's uncle's finca (farm). We had a conflict on whether to go to the cousin's wedding, or come here. I just did a painting, but I need to do some touching up. The painting is of the front of the farmhouse. Diana, her dad, and her aunt went to church. I'm here with her uncle Jairo. He is working on these number puzzles. He spends hours doing this for enjoyment. We came here around eleven, ate lunch, and then I had the rare occasion to take a nap. It's very nice here; the only problem is that it is on a major highway into Medellin, the same highway we take into the airport. It is located at the crest of the mountain. A few hundred feet away is the pass which leads into the town of Gruane where Diana's brother lives. Music from the 1940's is playing, the traffic is howling by, and I'm back somewhere in time in Colombia.

Yesterday we went to a million places shopping and completing errands. I was exhausted from all the walking. When we arrived home at Diana's parent's house, another uncle Fabio came by with his wife. We showed them the pictures of Costa Rica on the computer.

The walk to Diana's house at night was very interesting. It was our first time out at night, it was a Friday night, and the main street (La Playa) was hopping with activity. The street was packed with people. The cafes were filled and music was blaring everywhere. Street musicians and street acts were evenly spaced down the boulevard. The sidewalk was lined, almost to an impasse, with blankets on the ground filled with goods for sale. The smell of marijuana was everywhere and the city was very festive. I thought this street was wild during the day, but at night a terrific spectacle of life, art, and hocking takes place. The handcrafts were interesting to look at but most of these items are in every bizarre around the world.

One interesting facet of life here is the cell phone hocking on the street. No they are not selling the phones, they are selling calls. Men and woman stand by the hundreds wearing black vests that have phones hanging on chains. They look like bikers. Hanging on another chain is the price of the call per minute. This is in black ink or marker on a small poster around twelve inches by twelve inches. Sometimes a seller is standing there and three or four customers are speaking on cell phones chained to him or her. It's a nice inventive way of using technology and commerce.

I'm amazed at the hocking. A man or woman could be selling one item, spending the entire day doing this. How do so many people sell and make enough money to eat. How often do they change to a different commercial item, and how do they find this particular item to sell and why? I'm fascinated by business. I never like selling anything including my art and music. I wasn't in a position of real need, exactly, but there were times my rent money came from my artistic efforts. Too often I was financially between a rock and a hard place. To think that people all over the world eat depending on the income of that days endeavors baffles me.

Life here and in Costa Rica is how I envision a truly free economy should be in the United States. What happens in the United States is a counter-culture where life is pretty bleak when selling on the street, or at craft fairs. The legal bureaucracy of starting a business is very restrictive. I lived hand to mouth for a good portion of my life. It was very hard. The money needed to begin a business by renting a location is overwhelming for most people to really make it. There were times when I was a student that I felt raped by the system of education because of the financial burden. There were times I felt I would have done better under a communist government where the arts were supported. I'm sure Diana feels the same frustrations being an immigrant. There is no way around the sweat and toil if you are a businessperson or a student. I think I'm giving Diana a leg up on things whether she realizes it or not. This is one of the gifts I want to give to her.

People here and in the third world live more free than expressed by the propaganda of corporate media. The American life style is very confining and pretty rigid. As a teacher I feel like I can live like I want to a few months in the year. Our system of taxing and licensing stifles free living, and at the same time gives us a standard of living that is unsurpassed. I find the topic of economics and politics something I am quit opinionated about. Really, to me it's a mystery of how capitalism is based on greed and communism is based on suppression. We need something in between to really save the world. Could it be Socialism? The middle ground seems correct to me. (Yes, this is a bit simplistic.)

Forth Entry: This morning we took Tuto to the hospital. He was vomiting blood and had severe stomach pains. He has stomach ulcers. The household was in a panic, which makes me detach because I believe the time to be calm is when someone is ill. Diana and her mother are all wound up while Tuto is calm and making jokes. Having seen so much illness in my own parents doesn't make me get upset now. Maybe it's the way men and woman handle different situations. I see the need to attend to the ill as a process that doesn't leave room for emotion. My Latin wife is all emotions this morning. It is good we are here. Diana would be even more worried if we were elsewhere. I waited in the hospital for a couple of hours, and then Diana asked me if I wanted to go home. I walked here alone with no problems; in fact I took a few minutes to stop in the park.

Last night we were in the same park, right next to the apartment. It is the first week in August and there are preparations for the up-coming festival weekend. It is the Festival of Flowers. We will be in Bogotá and I made a mistake by booking our passage before the event. I'll miss not seeing the parade of flowers. I hear it is spectacular. The park last night was full of people selling in booths. The goods were typical Colombian wears, some cloths, jewelry, and lots of foods. We sat and Diana's mother spoke with some military troops. They are in the city to protect people while the festival takes place. It is a nice break for them to be around people. I half listened in as they spoke. They patrolled the park with loaded automatic weapons and the people take it in as if nothing is new. The park was certainly safe and the people enjoyed the moment very much. Children sit in carts that are painted to look like trains or cars. A man pushes the children around the park square, but they are oblivious to who is driving and powering their ride. The children sit and turn the steering wheel round and round. It's a serious, but fun, time for them. Music is being pumped through a public address system as singers stand on stage, but the music isn't live and the people don't even clap. A few drunken men dance in front of the singers, but they are in their own world, miles way from the audience that is indifferent. We laughed at the whole thing.

During the day we were at the finca. Diana's uncle, aunt, their son, and son's male lover came for lunch. Diana warned me not to ask any questions. She doesn't know me well enough yet. We all walked up into the property and had a nice visit. At one point we all sat on the ground and took pictures. I see how natural these people are and wonder why on earth anyone would want to be like the Americans. I saw the aunt hugging a tree and knew I was with the right kind of people.

When we returned to the house everyone sat around and talked as old time music played on a CD. It was heavenly to be in such a stress-free place and with such genuinely nice people. The pace of the day was calm, friendly, which is what we all need in our souls. I painted a good watercolor and visited with the folks off and on. At lunch Diana's uncles had a good laugh at me eating an avocado on bread. I wasn't about to put cold avocado into hot soup like they would have me do.

In the morning we caught a bus to Guarne, the little town where Diana's brother lives. The bus ride was ten minutes. The town square was filled with people and the Festival of Flowers was taking place. The actual flowers are not on display until the coming weekend, but the party is on all week. The festival is homage to life as it used to be. People dress in tradition cloths and eat foods that are traditional. The main parade has a showing of antique cars as well as the display of Flowers, which men carry on their backs on huge wooden planks. I've only seen photographs. The planks of flowers symbolize the days when the Spaniards were carried on the back of the indigenous people with chairs strapped to their backs.

At Diana's brothers house her cousin, his wife, and their two children were there visiting for the night. They had been at the wedding of another cousin the day before. Later, Fabio, Diana's uncle, and his wife stopped in. We sat around and talked while the children played games on the computer. The two sons' of Felipe never interact with anyone. They live on the computer. We've visited them in the States before and the same lack of interaction was present. I can't help but wonder what these new computer kids will be like. They will be highly skilled at technology, but lack communication skills. Who knows? We had to return to Uncle Juiro's house, so we returned to the town square just in time to catch a bus back to the finca. I enjoy all these people very much. No one is competing. My perception is that acceptance is more important than calculating and analyzing each other.

Third world people live more like my youthful hippie dream. In my early twenties I visited a couple of communes to see if I might fit in. The Farm in Tennessee and Harbon Hot Springs in California's Napa Valley both attracted me, but I never went full force into the life-style enough to give up my middle class needs. I was searching for a better tomorrow that came to me anyway. But I still feel the need to shun many of the middle class values I love to hate. The real struggle to survive gives one more dignity than being spoiled and pampered. Street life always had a romantic appeal to me. Camping on the land was my ultimate goal when I was young. I created my hippie-farm in Nebraska, my own way. I actually lived there with roommates on and off, but most of that time I was alone and doing creative works in art, music, and photography. There is something timeless to growing ones own food, not waking up to an alarm clock, and living a secluded life. The ability to be happy with what is right in front of you is an even greater gift. I spent three days without looking at the TV here. I thought that was a miracle. Last night I watched bits and pieces of English movies and I knew I wasn't missing a dam thing. I turned off the movies before they ended because I know the plots, and twists and turns they take anyway. Dare I say I want an unscripted life?

Diana is still at the hospital and Morelia (Diana's mother) had made me a nice lunch of rice, chicken and hot soup without avocado.

Fifth Entry: Yesterday we had many little fights. At one point I almost just left her on the metro. But there was no reason to make matters worse. The pressure she is under had made her mood sour. I don't have much patience for whining and self-pity. Except when it is in me! Diana feels tremendous influence to be financially supportive of her father. She feels guilt and is more often, more motivated by guilt than any other emotion. This makes me very angry. When I should have more compassion, I get verbal and start to lecture, which is not what she needs. But when she directs some of that madness at me I won't tolerate it. The family and the "responsibility" it imposes won't manipulate me.

Last night Diana's mother was feeling my hair and asking me to cut my hair. I asked Diana to ask her mother if I had ever suggested she cut her hair or dress any particular way. (This all took place in the hospital room). I got this little lecture back about how in Colombia it is the tradition to make suggestions (Actually openly criticize others with sugar coating). I asked Tutu if he ever told his wife to cut her hair. "Yes, I do these things to help her." Which was total bullshit, because the man isn't allowed to fart in the house without being told where to fart. My mood is sour too.

The day before in the hospital Diana asked me if I wanted a drink of Seven-up. I said no. Morelia saw this. She was present not more than a few feet away. Less than five minutes pass and Morelia asks me three times if I wanted a drink of Seven-up. I don't drink American soft drinks with sugar. I've taken one drink of Coke while here and that I didn't finish. Morelia tries to manipulate her daughter, anyone, and me with kindness. She is very sweet and soft-spoken, but very manipulative. Diana in turn, thinks I'm too strict and said yesterday I was like a stone wall. I don't waste my emotions. I don't have any control over anyone else but me. I prefer to call a spade a spade. I won't take a drink just to be nice. I won't follow a custom just to be nice.

The household is run like a tight ship. If I leave a camera or something out when I get home it has been replaced in another area by Morelia. This is my stuff in Diana's room, yet the mother goes in and rearranges her daughters' things. To me this is a red flag of danger, and very symbolic of deeper issues taking place in Diana's life.

The very religious aunt was visiting in the hospital and the Catholic mass came on TV. I was reading a book and continued to read it. I'm sure they had no clue why I was reading a book (on spirituality as a matter of fact) as the Mass was on. They all stood and repeated the prayers in a solemn mood. At one point I was reading how belief systems that are humorless, and dictatorial, are very dangerous to the spirit. Putting the guilt of Christ's death on the shoulders of the masses is a pretty heavy load. But even worse, and a perversion of all Christ's suffering, is to allow war and to continue to build churches with gold.

This morning I had a conversation with Diana about all the "customs", and how I felt it was a pile of poop. Many people have followed tradition into war and death. Yet those who refuse to be a part of this madness are considered heartless and looked down by the "true followers". When Diana married me she didn't know my belief system would come into conflict with hers and her family. She expected many of the traditional trappings of wealth and family. I don't think she will comprehend her own liberation for years. It takes all the courage one can muster to swim up-stream while the world is floating on a raft in the opposite direction.

I attend mass because I see how important it is to Diana. Is there an element of hypocrisy in my actions, maybe slightly, but more important is the need to share spiritual activity with my wife on her terms. I don't want to change her, but I do want to freely converse with what I see as important spiritual concepts. It has gotten me into trouble all my life because I have distinct views and try to live by my values every day. I learned a long time ago not to let others decide what was correct for me. Marriage doesn't have to change that. If I can't be true to myself I can't be true to the marriage. I sure won't let what is expected of me get in the way of what I see as correct. This is my strength and it comes across as strong, opinionated, and emotional. There are many slow poisons in life. They all come sugarcoated with wonderful immediate emotional gratification.

We visited three friends yesterday. One I'd never met before, she was six months pregnant. The topic of having babies came up at all three visits. One of the women is older and her children are grown. The other two are not married and have children or are about to have the first. I explained that I want to know my wife better and take things slow. Yet I find it strange that these women aren't married, have children, and live with their mothers. Yes, God does provide for us all, but there is nothing wrong with planning to support the child, and more importantly build the basis of a strong relationship with commitments. Once again tradition is seemingly more important than being practical. The woman are extremely nice people, they are important friends to Diana. I have nothing critical to say about their friendships, but the power of creation isn't a power that should be taken lightly. Having a cute doll to play with isn't my idea of being a provider. I see a responsibility first, but that can change.

Entry Six: We are about to leave for Bogotá and Ecuador. Diana had to shower after cleaning the house. These are two daily rituals that MUST be completed. Even the days Diana's mother was away at the hospital with Tuto the entire house was cleaned; swept, moped, and dusted. The outside streets are dirty, not as bad as Costa Rica, but the interior life here is spotless.

I've decided to leave the computer here for weight and safety reasons. I have a notebook that I'll use and re-enter the new writings when we get back to Medellin. I doubt that there will be time once we return to New York and teaching begins. The iPod and external speakers are a must to bring.

Last night the phone was ringing nonstop and the house had several visitors now that Tuto is back home from the hospital. A few people from the building stopped by, as well as the aunt and uncle.

We had a very nice day yesterday. The warring is over. Diana leaned into me and asked me for hugs several times. There is a cycle to relationships that one just has to be patient about. Our day started by cleaning, I do the writing, and Diana does the house. We left around noon, went and got $200 out of the bank, and went to see if there were some more Japanese dolls and wall hangings in a department store called Flamingo. I've bought two trinkets for Costa Rica, a small doll and wall hanging, both of Japanese women. The theme of the house in Costa Rica is the Orient, so there are lots of things from the Chinese import stores. I've tried to narrow all this down to the Orient because the house in New York is full of world trinkets.

The day was directionless, all walking, and a brilliant way to spend our last day here in Medellin. I love that kind of wandering. We went to the cities commercial center, which is block upon block of tiny shops inside of shopping centers. The most prevalent items are woman's clothes. There are very few handmade crafts, which is what interests me. I could buy 99% of the goods here in New York. I look for art or crafts that exhibit the real past, the way people carved with their hands, or made something with love. It amazes me where all the goods come from, and more importantly where all the unsold items end up. Does this stuff end up in the junk heap? There's no way that all these goods are sold. How much does business contributes to the world's pollution problem, not to mention how much food is wasted each day that is sent to the dump.

I haven't kept exact track of the amount of money we've spent, but we have a four thousand dollar budget left. I hope to save half of that for the extra room we are building in the apartment when we return to New York. I don't see how we can spend even two thousand dollars. I think we've spent around two thousand plus, but much of that was for the house in Costa Rica. I had $1,300 set aside for house improvements. I spent around $900; the largest expense was the new windows. I'll do a cost analysis when we return and I can see all the bank and credit card transactions. I go online to check the accounts. The biggest expense is the airline tickets, and they were paid for months ago.

I hope to buy some handmade crafts in Ecuador; the market here isn't as arty as I'd hoped. The same goes with Costa Rica, but I've bought some nice vests and belts there with touches of Guatemalan handy craft. The shops in Jaco have lots of items that are handcrafts, but that is because the tourists buy that kind of thing. The prices are outlandish in Jaco because of this. I'm looking for a simple wooden bowl here, but that isn't so easy to find. I saw them on the bus one day on the way to La Ceja. I couldn't stop the bus.

I'm excited to go. It is a little stale after being here in the parents house. I feel like there are lots of other places to see in Colombia. Life in any city becomes predictable. Life with others, and not being in ones own home is not easy because of a lack of privacy. The two days Morelia was in the hospital with Tuto gave me a window of time to pack and get myself prepared for the traveling to come. Last night I went to bed early, put on the iPod, and drifted away with my thoughts. That was nice. Diana was cleaning the house with her mother. The traffic here is nonstop even though we are five floors up from the street. The wind blows through the place very well because we are high off the street. Quiet here isn't anything like quiet in Long Island, New York where the birds and our backyard are a sanctuary. Every once in a while I miss home, but I'll get there. Yesterday Diana said she wanted to just go home. The pressure of being around the family is greater than she knows. At one point she was crying because she felt bad for not helping her father with the hospital bills. "What can I do, he is my papa?" I haven't felt like my parents were my responsibility since I left because of the violence alcoholic behavior when I was seventeen. I see my attitude as being able to conserve my emotions and money for myself first. Who knows, we are attracted to that which we need.

Chapter 12. Ecuador

Ecuador was amazing to me. I did not bring the computer for writing, but jotted down some notes here and there. The only plan that remained the same after our arrival was to see Quito, originally we were to go south and see the volcanoes and hot springs. We made plans to visit a woman who works with Diana in school, but were unable to reach her by phone. However, we talked to her sister and mother, and when travel dates were changed we were forced to make new plans.

Upon landing, we hired a taxi at the airport to take us to the hotel but on arriving there realized that conditions at the hotel were terrible. The room was fifteen dollars a night, which was somewhat expensive so we drove to a few more hotels, also very expensive. In spite of the price, they were all fully booked so we chose the fourth hotel, which was like finding a gold mine. We arrived late at night. The room was large with three beds, but very noisy. It was on the second floor above a street with drunks and people scuffling about late into the night.

The next day we asked for a room off the street. For thirty-eight dollars a night we switched to a suite across from the sauna. It was scented with fresh eucalyptus branches, a whirlpool, and steam room. They told us we could use the sauna anytime so we took advantage of some late night therapeutic visits. Although the bedroom had no windows, it was up another flight of stairs and was like a palace. The room was all brick with large half dome arches. It was very quiet and that night we slept peacefully. The door never properly locked but we felt safe. The hotel itself seemed very secure. In the mornings, we would eat our breakfast in a sunny, inner court with plants hanging from the hotel balconies above. A small fountain trickled in the center of the courtyard; and small shops lined the ground floor. The visiting guests were from every corner of the globe. The room was at our disposal for three days, before the big rush of people coming in for the weekend. The hotels were all booked because of the Independence Day celebrations. We decided to enjoy our good fortune and not worry about leaving until the weekend. The hotel clerks were young and well spoken and the man who worked the night desk had visited the United States and had family in Connecticut.

When I think of Quito one thing comes to mind, churches. Not ordinary churches, but the most exquisite architectures I have ever seen. These buildings of ornate detail and design, especially the altars, were as beautiful as churches in Rome. The influence is Spanish and Moorish. A number of the churches were under renovation, but the condition of many of them was well preserved. It left me in a state of awe. I have been to Europe several times and seen many churches around the world, but Quito should be the considered the capitol of Catholic churches.

One church that is a must to see is the Monastery of San Francisco. The church is under guard because of the overwhelming amount of gold visible on every area of its surface. There are two colors in this church, gray on the exterior, and gold on the inside. I cannot begin to describe the elaborate ornate designs that spun, swirled, and lifted the eye onto the dome. Gold leaf covered the carved, intricate patterns and where the gold leaf ended and solid gold began was impossible to ascertain. I was videotaping when I heard a voice in Spanish tell me they did not permit this. When we exited the church, the authorities stopped us and asked that we show our payment receipts, which we did not have not knowing this was required. They escorted us back inside and paid a small fee. I was indignant that I needed to pay to visit God. However, as a new visitor in their country I left peacefully.

The Plaza of Independence was further down the street. To get there we passed another church, which I assumed might be older and less beautiful. Yes, it was older, but so breathtakingly beautiful I gasped for breath. They were performing renovations on the church yet the flow of praying visitors was constant. We must have seen ten equally beautiful churches that day. I was astonished to see so many exquisite houses of God. Why in Ecuador? Why had I not heard about such incredible architectural wonders? Once again, one can only attend the University of Life while traveling.

We spent three days in the old town of Quito and wandered to wherever we could see a church steeple or museum. My cameras were always rolling. What I want to photograph is totally unscripted, dependent on the light, and equally spontaneous. We started in local commercial areas, strolled into quiet neighborhoods until we came to busy shopping areas again. We had no plans and I like it exactly that way. I had a Lonely Planet book, which we used at first, but quickly saw the major attractions because the old town is small, maybe a few square miles. We did a little shopping and a couple of hours away traveling by bus came across the small town of Otovalo, where one can find finely crafted Indian handicrafts. I landed some good bargains because I know to ask before spending a lot of money in the typical tourist shops (traps). Unless an item is very rare, I wait before I buy.

The second biggest impression of Ecuador is the Indians. They are a separate people that stand out because of their traditional dress. The Indian men wear white shirts and white pants with white shoes that are a kind of slipper. They always have a poncho draped over one shoulder, and wear a hat. The women are more colorful and wear beautifully floral, embroidered white blouses with lots of lace around the neck and sleeves. Their skirts are black and made of heavy wool. Around their necks are many strands of small gold beads and on their heads they wear shawls folded in a manner that keeps the sun from their eyes. If you did not know, you would think these were hats. After the sun passes over the mountains, these shawls act as a source of warmth. The street edges are lined with Indian woman and men selling a variety of goods. The sellers passively call out to the passersby. They sell everything from fruits and vegetables, to cloth. The Indians have a silent dignity to them. Though poor they are dignified because of their dress and how well kept their hair and clothes are. They do not shower every day, but that is because of the cold weather. They are proud and beautiful.

A third image remains in my mind about Ecuador. We were riding in a bus back from our five-day stay in Otovalo, where a one-lane landslide closed the road partially. Three men with wheelbarrows and shovels were moving the dirt. This would take them at least three days. This lack of equipment puts the country on the level of Stone Age labor. The man with the truck was standing "supervising" the event. All over the world, there is shared labor and in the United States, there might be three supervisors and four laborers.

On the bus ride into Otovalo, we sat with a man and his grandchild. Diana asked him about his family. She wanted to know where he lived. He said he was a farmer and had gone to see another of his sons in Quito and brought along his grandchild. Sometimes I don't like to spoil the encounter with anything but friendly words. The cameras seem inappropriate and exploitive on some occasions. When something pure comes your way, you don't want to leave a fingerprint. I only want to leave a glimmering beautiful exchange that can only repeat in my memory. When nothing tangible remains, not even a face to recall, the experience has the capacity to circle back around in a surprise memory. This man was wonderful and full of love for his grandchild. He was forty-five, but he looked sixty to me. I was astonished at his weathered hands and mostly impressed with his open heart. He was wise enough to size up anyone on the planet. He wasn't looking for demons in others, just smiles and a friendly chat to pass the ride.

I can't explain the connections I felt with these people. It wasn't like driving through Arizona and seeing the shantytowns of Indians. These Indians live a culture that is continuous for many generations. They were invaded but not conquered. The dignity shines through in their traditional dress. They aren't cowboys in blue jeans, so much as Indians in Indian clothes. The vast number of Indians wearing their traditional clothes gives a much different impression than the defeated culture that is slowly gaining back it's pride in the American South-West. I don't claim to give a fair assessment of something I only see from an outsiders point of view, but I genuinely was feeling more interest and love from these strangers than I've felt in my own country. This may be from many factors, but I often wonder about the generational scars of slavery and defeated tribes in the United States verses peoples who were never stripped of their dignity by conquering governments. These invisible racial separations lay deep in the psyche of every child, even the supposed well-off white suburban child. Dignity produces children that want to learn, verses children who feel they are forced to learn. I was in the later group and resented what was being taught to me by my elders.

The first morning we arrived in Otovalo we were awakened by the sound of rocks being hand-tossed into a tractor bucket, one bomb at a time. We didn't know what it was until I looked out the curtains to see men working in the street below. The stonework was labor intensive and each brick was placed by hand into the puzzle on the sidewalk. While later walking down the street we noticed small children playing, or helping their father in a play-like activity. The fathers brought their children to their job site and stay with them all day as each man earns a living. How many lawyers would it take in the United States to allow such an activity where parents bring children to a job? I see something beautiful in this. I see the children learning the value of work. I see the fathers allowing the children to help hold dustpans of shovels because it is natural to want to help. When a child sees others working, they join in. The glue that holds a family together is a common approach to life. We can't turn back the clock in the United States, but there is something seriously lacking in the manor families are no longer a laboring unit, but an entertainment unit.

We spent the first day just walking and photographing in the small town. The market was the most interesting. It was in a central sector that was a hog-pog of building with long corridors. In the middle was a big section of open-air restaurants where wooden stools lined counter tops with people eating. The food was all out in the open, pork heads with their mouths open, but fully cooked, sides of cooked beef, and the smell of delicious vegetables. We ordered a glass of raw carrot juice mixed with wheat grass. The health benefits out weighted the lack of sanitation. I suppose some people would shutter at such a non-hygienic atmosphere, but really, for thousands of years we lived in natural settings without chemicals that killed any and everything. It dawned on me that the trends in natural foods in recent years were something that never existed in this place I was visiting. What we think is "new" is really ancient and common wisdom. I know the bulk of the food there is grown without chemicals. I felt like I was in a food heaven where the abundance of healthy and natural food, was very obvious.

Because of commercialism in the United States, ancient concepts get reinvented, packaged, and promoted as "new", but this is a type of false cultural illusion. Much of the basic beliefs of the sixties and seventies that were new to my generation were really ancient. In an atmosphere of being reintroduced as "new and radical", the principles were actually timeless. What was "new" was the young people and how they interpreted other cultures. "Hippieism" was a way to culturally ingest the mannerisms of third world living. The Hippies rejected a highly commercial and regimented life. Sharing resources, sharing living spaces, traveling and making pilgrimages, entering into spiritual states of mind, and growing ones own food, have been a part of all cultures. This back to basics movement threatened mainstream life because it shunned commercialism. What greater threat to Capitalism than not having consumers? My Catholic upbringing was so restricted, and strict, I was attracted to open religions like Hinduism and Buddhism. These religions addressed living with greed and avarice. The culture of the Indians in Ecuador interests me deeply. What some might call "primitive", I would call long standing communities. I had little to observe beyond the surface, except in the handicrafts, art, and a communal sweat lodge I happened upon.

We stayed for two days in a small hotel when we asked the owners if they knew of a hotel close, but in the countryside. The man named John offered to take us to his house where he had several rooms for rent. We had seen the town of Otovalo and pretty much canvassed every street by then. John took us in his truck to his house about ten minutes out of town. The room was sparse made of natural furniture and local fabrics hung as curtains and bedspreads. The kitchen was a strange room because the place for cooking didn't seem to be the focus. A portion of the expansive room had a loom sitting in the middle. It was very primitive and a real house where many people lived, not a hotel as such. John said there were students living in some of the rooms. I asked to use the restroom. This is a way to really see what one is getting into. The toilet was a hole in the ground that was in the back of the house. It had no doors and was an open-air stall. That was all I needed to know. The shower was an open air booth with an electric heater visible right next to the toilet area. This was the only source of hot water in the house. I went back to the main room and looked at Diana. She read my expression. They kept inviting us even after we said we wanted to try something else. The topper to this situation was John asking us for five dollars when we returned to the hotel. I paid him, but was not happy with the sudden change from a hospitable friend to a conniving businessman. The five dollars was well worth an avoided vacation disaster.

We went straight to our room in the hotel and packed up the suitcases. We took our luggage to the lobby and asked them if it was ok to leave it there until we made arrangements to leave in a few hours. I had seen a travel agency a few blocks away while we walked the town. We headed straight there and met a husband and wife who had their small child in a crib. They were wonderful and very accommodating. There was a nice place ten minutes away that was in the country and sounded very good. The price was the same as the other hotel, something like twenty-two dollars a day. We called and made a reservation, got the address, and went back to the original hotel. We told them we were going back to Quito, just to be more diplomatic about the refusal of their offer to stay in their home. On the curb the hotel clerk who helped us move the bags to the street said he would take us to the bus station. I caught the eye of the driver and put a finger over my lips because I secretly said we were going to another hotel. He caught my drift instantly.

We drove a few minutes and found we were heading in the same direction that John had taken us. The taxi driver took us up toward the mountains base, down a dirt road that had abandoned railroad tracks, and to a beautiful hotel that was all white with the rooftops covered in straw. The all white hotel was separated into many buildings; a restaurant was on one side of the track as the bulk of the sleeping rooms were on the other side. The office was on the same level as the train tracks, and down a flight of stairs was an open courtyard. Another set of stairs took us even deeper to a small creek with hammocks hanging in the trees. It was a small sanctuary with a shrine and trees that shaded the area. We liked it instantly.

The owner was a Dutch woman who married a local Indian man. She had been there for twenty plus years. The next morning she gave us a ride into town and we exchanged stories. She was a hippie who left her country to see the world and found love in this distant place. Her two children (sons) were living in Holland and going to school. Her husband was a short man with a slow pace. While riding into town I told her about the other hotel owner charging us money to show his house and give us a ride. She agreed it wasn't a nice thing to do. As it turned out, John's house was a few blocks away from this Hotel. John never mentioned it and we asked several times if he could find us a hotel in the country. Diana pointed the house out to me when we were walking on the second day. I didn't see anyone recognizable, but it was the same place we had been brought. Now I was more in love with the hotel than ever. I also know that in these small towns every one knows every one else and word would eventually get back to John that we stayed in the white hotel. I love these kinds of weaving connections.

I'm writing in retrospect. Most of it stays in my mind. On the first day in the country hotel we walked to a near by waterfall. It was a weekend and there were many families in a festive mood. We stayed a little while, laying in the deep grass, and walked back to the hotel. I wanted to do some painting so I took off before sunset. Diana stayed in the room and read a book on the early French explorers who came to Ecuador. I crossed a dry river bed on a tiny footbridge and went up a brick path that emerged into a communal courtyard where a low sauna stood. I exited the courtyard to a dirt path. Close by I found a mound of earth and set up my watercolors. Soon there was a small troop of local children surrounding me and asking me what I was doing. I was delighted to have such wonderful company. It is easy to communicate with the small children, and fun besides.

We ran into these same children and their family several times during our stay. One night we heard music so we went into the hotel restaurant. There a band of young men were playing traditional music with flutes, drums, guitars, and mandolins. Some of the musicians and dancers were from the family we had met while I was painting. I think there were eight children all together. One morning Diana and I went over the small creek, up the embankment to the dirt path that led past this family's home. It was morning and many chores were taking place. The children were finished with a bath and getting their hair combed. The tears and fuss was no different from any child in the world resisting the pain of a comb through their wet hair. I took a few photographs and felt honored to be invited into their lives. The father of the group showed me his hand-loom and how it functioned. Three hours for one knit scarf is the fastest it went for him. His mother had a small hut in the front of the property. Across the dirt path they had a large, beautiful strawberry patch with chickens running about eating insects. The field was labor intensive. Everything was done by hand. I doubt that any pesticides were applied to the crop.

The dirt floors in the house and the children in their bare feet was a stark difference to what we were accustomed to. Other than the children and their running noses, life seemed to be healthy and good. But they were very poor. The man asked me to buy a scarf, but I declined. The day we were leaving I gave them some money. The product they were selling didn't appeal to me.

On another occasion I went out to shoot photographs in the afternoon. I walked quite a distance along the base of the mountain. I was following the irrigation channel that came from the mouth of the waterfalls we had previously visited on the first day. I was in a place that not many tourists, if any, had ever been. Small farms lay on both sides of the small channel. Primitive wooden bridges crossed the irrigation channel to these farms. At one point I saw a woman coming toward a bridge. She had a large sickle in her hand. My first instinct was to see if she was coming toward me. Looking over my shoulder, I soon realized she was only on the path long enough to walk down the embankment into a field. I said hello, and in an unusual scene, she did not say anything to me. I was very foreign and strange to her.

Eventually I found a dirt road and headed down toward the houses. As I passed one field an old woman and her grandchild were in a dried field picking beans. The Indians share their crops with those who don't have enough. The idea of private property is outweighed by the needs of the community. Some of the houses had a rumbling sound coming from inside. At one house I stood in the courtyard door listening. I was there a long time and suddenly a short man appeared at the door to his courtyard. I spoke in broken Spanish; I was wondering what all the noise was. He invited me inside the courtyard and into a small room. To my amazement, two huge machines sat there like iron monsters. The noise I had heard was an electric loom. He gave me a demonstration. The wires that lead to the wall were exposed and everything looked like it would break down at any second. One of the two machines was running. The second sat idol, as well as a third machine outside under a tin roof that was also a kind of front porch. That machine was not in use. I assume the machines got old and newer machines were replacing the smaller older ones. The room with the newer machines was an add-on, built to house them. What can one do with a machine that wears out? Leave it. It's like having a small junk tractor just sitting there. There is no place to vacate such a large albatross.

Soon family members came to see who was talking with the elder. I sat on a small box and they showed me some beautiful shawls. I didn't really want anything, but bought two, one black and one gold. They gave me a third smaller scarf as a gift. The son of the elder introduced me to his sister and wife. Several small children were popping up wondering who the traveler was. All together fifteen people lived in the compound. I took many photographs and was very happy to just be there in the midst of such common and natural people. Such events make me humble. The son with one child holding his hand walked me to the road that lead back to the hotel.

The next morning Diana and I returned to the same family. This time there were many more people present. We asked them to see more shawls. They obliged and we bought ten. We decided to buy a quantity and give them as gifts to our friends. Diana hit it off well with them, as she does with most people. We later sent them photographs via the Internet. I am embarrassed to say how little we paid for the shawls. I am sure we gave them a good price, yet these same objects would sell for ten times as much in the States. How lucky I am to have met these people, as short as it was. Today I feel touched in the heart by our encounter, all because of a noisy machine.

The Saturday market was the big draw for most of the tourists. It was no disappointment. Street after street of goods filled the imagination. For me, the more natural and realistic the item the more I am attracted to it. We bought small nativity scenes, a collar-less shirt, a few sweaters, and an orange rug for the matching floor tiles in Costa Rica. Diana, of course, bought some jewelry. I kept telling her all summer to wait until we got to Ecuador to buy things. The prices were great. I have a few tactics while buying; one is that I must get a bargain out of the seller. If they reach that point of aggravation on their face I know I've taken them to their limit. This is something I learned in Iran and Pakistan when I was a teenager. We met two sisters from New York in a café and they said they felt at a loss when it came to know how to negotiate. I told them, half the opening price and begin from there. This may have been a bit steep, but I saw them buying later. They had smiles that affirmed less anxiety about buying in a situation that has no marked price tags.

Our biggest and most important purchase turned into a long drawn out ordeal. We wanted six identical fabrics to make into curtains and a bedspread. In the morning I had found a woman who was willing to negotiate with me, so I returned near market closing time to see if we could work out a better agreement. She remembered me and exactly where we had left off in the negotiations. The only problem was she could not give me the same run of fabric all at the same length. There were some slight differences, so we agreed that I'd come back in the morning, first thing. The poor woman had her brother and everyone else running looking for the correct match. When we came back in the morning they still could not get us six. We said we would return again, but we looked further a few blocks away. In this stall a young girl and her father told us they would get us five fabrics and a sixth fabric with the additional length. The girl told us how most people selling in the market cheated on the longer fabric by telling the buyer it was a full meter long when it wasn't. I believed her. We waited maybe an hour before the red faced young girl came through for us. Even though I had negotiated her down to the nearest nickel I added in a few extra dollars to thank her for her efforts. We took photographs of the two merchants. We were all happy with the good deal.

The fabrics and all our purchases were packed away into an extra suitcase we bought for thirty dollars. The new luggage broke within five minutes. I'm forever buying cheap luggage that lasts as long as the trip. The best and most efficient "luggage" I buy instead are plastic bags with zippers. They are made in China. These are a plaid pattern plastic bag that sells for a dollar. They are lightweight and come with handles. I reinforce the bags. I put one or two inside the other and then wrap the outside with duct tape. Even if I don't use one I always have an extra bag, or two, stuffed in the front pouch of my luggage for emergency carry on items. I brought along bubble wrap and skillfully pack breakable items inside the center, while clothes and new jackets surround the outer areas. It works well.

We spent a lot of time sewing and planning the curtains for a new room I built. I began before we left and finished the room a month ahead of schedule in October. We bought a sewing machine a year earlier and put it to good use, our first use, when we made the curtains, pillows, and bedspread. The fabrics are yellow with gold and beige lines running through. There are small Indian figures inside the design. The colors of the walls and the decor of the room were essentially based on these fabrics. Our tailoring isn't so perfect, but the energy we spent gathering and creating the curtains and bedspread is very precious. We are very proud of what we created together. I spent every day after work building the room. I did the drywall, and gutted the room before we left. There was years of junk and many things I had stored, like my motorcycle. Things got to a point that I was obsessed and sick of working, but all the fruits of my labors have paid off. Anyway, the curtains are up. I sewed the last pillowcases one morning at five AM. It's a very happy, golden room.

One day we hired a taxi from the city center to give us a half-day tour. The driver obliged and was a wonderful chap. He gave us his name and number, asking to hire us for the ride back to Quito, but we took the bus for two dollars instead. The bus ride was full of surprises, like the man next to Diana throwing up into a paper bag. The winding roads were too much for him. We did see a great movie with the Mexican superstar, Vicente Fernandez. I was intrigued by this early 1960's Mexican movie.

I had time to do a quick painting when the taxi driver took us to the top of a volcano. In the crater was a huge lake with an island in the middle. Small tour boats were the only indication of scale and showed us the immensity of this lake. We were high up and the air had a good chill. Off in the distant valley we could see the town of Otovalo. It was an alpine setting in a place that was characteristically non-alpine. The air was crisp and smelled of wonderful berries that lay at my knees as I painted. Diana and the driver visited as I painted and got the occasional passer bye that stopped to see what I was doing. We descended into a valley and the driver showed us the farm he had grown up on. He told Diana how he was working as a driver to support the family. I took video and wondered how on earth so many people all around the world work so hard to survive.

We drove into another small town where the specialty was leather goods. I wasn't at all interested in any cow products. Diana was a little disappointed in my wanting to leave, but we'd already bought her a jacket. I was more interested in the Town Square and beautiful blossoming pink trees than another store with tourists. The markets on the street spoil store shopping for me. But by the end of our nine days even the street markets were tiring. For me it's partly the emotional drain of so many futile sales pitches by the booth keepers. When we shop in a store it is impersonal. The streets are different. Only once was a seller nasty to us. I was looking at colors and sizes of rugs. The woman scurried about pulling things out and then running to the neighbors to get what she thought we wanted. But the color and sizes weren't what we wanted. As we walked away I knew she was swearing a blue streak at us. I had a particular item in mind. I found it a day later. The Indian people are generally sweet natured and downright humble, but this woman was having a bad day and let off some steam. It's so obvious the gringo's bring in three times what they might sell amongst themselves.

We left the last morning. We didn't have the usual confusion of asking where to catch the bus. The taxi driver knew which bus was the direct bus. This bus didn't go into the terminal. He explained that the bus would go by on the main highway just as we pulled onto that very road. Within a few seconds the bus we needed was already passing. I thought we had missed it, but the taxi driver bolted out into traffic and a fast chase ensued. He speed along side of the bus and gestured to the bus driver that two people wanted to get on the bus. The bus pulled over. Without a word being spoken we bought the two last seats, but not next to each other. We had one sick, vomiting, young man between us. It was real. Vicente Fernandez kept the entire bus glued to the screen the next two hours. The film star/ singer played the role of a gambler who loved his worst enemies wife. You don't need to speak Spanish to watch his movies. The visual story melodrama in their body language is enough to get the plot.

When we arrived back in Quito we caught a taxi to a hotel we found in our Lonely Planet book. We were no longer in the old town, but a newer part of the city. We settled in the room for a while, and then went out to eat and buy birth control pills. The pills were half what we'd spend in the States, so we bought a years supply. The restaurant was a fast food place specializing in seafood. It was a huge step above the typical fast food restaurants in the States. We ordered shrimp and rice. Afterwards we walked across a busy boulevard to a huge park with more crafts for sale. I didn't want to look at more so we just went to a grassy mound and lay down to relax. Lovers and the homeless sat around in the park.

The next morning we left for the airport early enough to be the second in line at the counter. This proved futile because our reservations were not honored and we spent an hour at a second ticket counter proving we had receipts and we indeed had reservations. Avianca is the worst airline in South America. The red tape and lack of organization is obvious. The attitude is that of an authoritarian, military-like organization where you are subject to endless questions and treated as a suspect. When Diana came to the United States they stole many of her things. They "confiscated" them because her luggage was over weight. They are bullies. We got on our flight but it was no easy task. Every time we leave Colombia we go through a process of searching the bags that is really a violation of our privacy. I feel the same about being searched in lines at any airport. Forfeiting my rights in the name of national security is a sign of the government's failure. I should not have to pay for any inconvenience. So much has been justified in the name of "9/11" that the public has become like sheep. The worst threat to freedom has come from within our governments.

We arrived back in Medellin after a quick transfer in Bogotá and more security nonsense. We walking around and around, when we could have walked directly off the airplane into the waiting room. We arrived home to Diana's mom and dad waving to us. We noticed that our bags didn't even go through customs when we arrived back in Colombia, nor back in Medellin. We took them off the carousel and walked right out of the airport. It was great to see Diana's parents. We were all in good sprits and did our typical stop at the roadside café overlooking the valley to

Medellin. I am a very lucky guy to have such a lovely wife and family.

Chapter 13. Colombian Journal Part 2.

It has been almost three weeks since I last wrote. Not that I lacked any inspiration, I've been busy traveling to Ecuador and spending time, a lot of time, with Diana and the family. The time included a quinceanera, a death, and the subsequent funeral, back, to back, to back. The uncle of Diana's sister in law died. The niece of the sister in law had a party for her fifteenth birthday: quinceanera. I have been attending these events with the family and doing daily activities since our return from Ecuador. For one day, we spent time with the niece and the next day with the nephew. It was for his birthday. We took him to lunch and an American animated movie in a shopping mall.

I do not know where to begin. I try to keep track of events with the journal but the days have blended into the struggles and joys of matrimony, and the struggles and joys of traveling. I go from extremes of just wanting to be alone to feeling deeply in love. The family wares me down in terms of the energy it takes to be around others. At one point, I said I just want to be alone, away from everyone, and be on a beach.

The biggest conflict came when Diana had her eye brows and eyelids tattooed. There is a custom here when the woman go to a special parlor and have their eyeliner permanently tattooed onto their eyelids. What follows is days of pain and torture, not to mention the possibility of a terrible infection setting in. As open minded as I think I am, I find this whole thing bazaar and stupid. When I walked into the room and saw Diana, I was really taken aback by her look. I am not, nor ever was, into women who wear a lot of makeup. However, Diana looked like a cross between Sophia Loren and Cleopatra (the Elisabeth Taylor version). The bruising made her eyes look like a wife beater had taken to her. It turned my stomach. Here my wife is saying, "Look how pretty I am!" I feel like she has been masochistic using her beauty as her tool.

I was with her aunt, Peidad, while Diana was in the salon. We had taken a long walk to Peidad's mother's and sister's house to fill the time for three hours. A couple of days later, I did not help matters by saying prostitutes painted their faces in such a manor. I have been assured that this ugly state will pass and a new beauty will emerge after the scars heal. I am still wondering why this is so important to her. The result is not to have to put on any eye make-up every morning, but the suffering and bruised look is terrible. Am I being insensitive?

That day we took off for Guarne around three o'clock in Tuto's little white Fiat. Five minutes into the drive, I knew there was trouble. The car dies if it idols, so Tuto constantly guns the engine which gives off an occasional "Boom, Boom" from backfiring. There was a long traffic backup on the cities major road and we had many near misses in the stop and go traffic. Tuto is maneuvering the hand brake, the foot brake, the accelerator, and the clutch in a series of motions not that different from the Wizard of Oz when he is discovered behind the curtain. "Pay no attention to this wild screaming car, I am the great Oz."

One day while on the same highway we saw a truck lose it's front wheel. The truck thumped to the ground and scraped a line of sparks across the concrete. The wheel bounced down a series of embankments, past cars and people playing in a park. No one was hurt. It was like watching a movie, only everyone escaped danger. (Unlike a Hollywood production) I was fully prepared to write a new chapter on disaster for our travels on this highway. A few minutes later, a woman on a moped stopped next to us and leaned into the car scratching it. She perhaps cracked her mirror, but she was gone before we could tell if any damage really took place to the moped or Tuto's car.

The entire time we were driving, rather crawling along in traffic, the car was dying. Tuto would either restart the engine by hand or let the clutch pop to re-ignite the motor. Every time the car died, the screaming engine caused looks of terror from neighboring cars. In addition, of course, Tuto would not stay in one lane. He is a lane hopper. We never got any further any faster, but he had this desire to feel he was at least moving somewhere. The worst and ultimate part of this experience was the pollution. The buses and trucks here are years away from keeping with air quality standards. I was sitting in the front seat being chocked to death by passing bus fumes. I was just beginning with the first signs of a flu and I am positive this sealed my fate from any possible faster healing. For a good forty-five minutes, we braved the traffic until we began the long climb out of the city on the road that leads to Gruane and the airport. Tuto commented to me that the car is fine once it leaves the traffic of the city.

This car has been the topic of many discussions in the family. Everyone but Tuto wants it dead and buried. He treasures this white elephant like a teenager with his first car. He has jimmy-rigged every imaginable concoction possible from storage compartments to new side panels that are held in with grommets. The car is a marvel and has outlived thousands of normal deaths. Any suggestion of buying a new car, or rather, new-used-car is ended with instant anger and attitude. He loves his car.

I know what happens in these circumstances because of my own history with cars. It is a kind of dysfunctional dance of chance and repair. After a while, the car is more important than life itself. So many repairs have extended it's driving life that expenses no longer even becomes a problem. Give the god damn car eternal life. Let it run even if it ruins everything else in one's life. I have had three or four such cars when I was in my worst economic state. Of course, the fact that every action has a subsequent reaction is based on "wrong thinking". It is like faith and religion. Believing is not seeing, believing is having the opportunity to trick the mind into what it wants to believe. No matter what obstacles, the screaming engine becomes the baby at baptism. Let the child cry because the soul is being saved. The roaring engine wears out the valves. The clutch is worn down so that has to be replaced. The brakes go from overuse. The carburetor is malfunctioning because the engine is constantly overheated and being gunned. There is life after death. It is just that tiny awkward moment before eternal salvation that gets in the way. What the hell! Give it more gas. Accelerate!

We arrived at the house in time to get to the mass for the girl of the quinceanera. The church is at least two hundred years old. The simple white walls were rolling uneven surfaces with dark, black rafters and exposed support beams. At the foot of the altar three chairs draped in light-green fabrics and flowers were reserved for the parents and their child. These chairs were for Paola, Carlos and Luz. They all three sat with their daughter in the middle. This family is related through Diana's sister in law. The solemn mass ended with a burst of applause as the young girl exited the church. We then walked in a line to a side building on the church grounds where the party was to take place. As we stood in line, a cow behind a barbwire fence stuck his head over the wires and sniffed at the people. No one seemed that alarmed by such a commonplace event. We stood in the cold as each guest signed the guest book. Before the signature, each person was handed a light-green drink of milk mixed with alcohol. Ah, the first drink of many that follow for most guests.

After a painful length of waiting time, the party began with the young woman being escorted into the hall by six white toy-like solders in tall black boots. She wore a light-green gown. Each step the uniformed participants took was well choreographed with an inner step of three leg swings before moving onto the next full step. The lead man is usually gay at these events. You ask why? Because they know how to dance, and more importantly, never hit on the young girl for sex. I wanted to say "bride" because this feels like a wedding. All right, you get the picture. The boots, the white tall hats, there is even a corridor of swords that create a hall, or passageway, for the young virgin queen to pass through. All is symbolic of the young girl's passage into adult life.

"Pomp and Circumstance", a little "Swan Lake" by Tchaikovsky, a bit of spice with Latino music, and the evening built into a festive explosion as a balloon burst with tiny colored paper raining down on the dancers. This was followed by a troop of young music makers who marched into the hall singing "Happy

Birthday" in English, or what they thought was English. The merry makers had a big drum made of cowhide, a set of bongos, a large horn, and lots of enthusiasm. They sang and banged through several traditional songs. Diana told me this was the music of the costal peoples. We ate dinner, had a few drinks. I was drinking straight rum to calm the gripa (flu) in my lungs. The rum put us in the mood to dance. There was rum, coke, and some kind of clear Colombian liquor that smelled like gasoline. I stuck to the rum. I know if I stay too long at such events I get very strung out, so I asked Diana if we could leave before the crowd was too drunk.

Francisco, Diana's brother, lives one block away. Actually, on the very next street with the back of his house on the very building we had attended the party. Therefore, the music was still alive as we lay down on the pullout sofa bed. This was a foam bed really. Right where the middle of my back lay there was a two by four for reinforcement. I know this bed from one time before. It is in a room that includes the kitchen and a small sun porch. I did not fall asleep for hours. In the mean time, Fabio came home and told Diana that the uncle had died. We had plans in the morning to do a driving tour of some small towns. We would attend the funeral the very next day, and then leave for the finca. The plan to see many small towns was axed. We had to attend the funeral.

The next morning Tuto and I were the only ones awake. Therefore, he asked me to go get a bunuelo. This is a donut that is a round ball without any hole, they are delicious and a common item here in Colombia. It was around six in the morning. The streets were empty until we reached the town square. At the gate of the little park stood several drunks. At least nine men were leaning and fumbling into each other. They did not see us; they were occupied by their state of drunken bliss. Tuto and I went into a little restaurant and I had a rare cup of coffee, I never drink the stuff. At one point three of the drunks stumbled into the restaurant. People noticed them but it seemed to be an event common for a Sunday morning. One man was particularly drunk and not able to keep his balance. The other two helped, but they were not in much better shape to walk. Maybe five minutes went by when the very drunk man tried to run out of the restaurant with the other two following in wobbly pursuit. People stopped to look just long enough to take the next sip of coffee.

Tuto took me to the new commercial center. It was several blocks in the opposite direction of the house. He was describing what I thought would be a shopping center. It looked like one from the outside, more or less. It was a big two-story building. In front of the building was the remaining flower displays from the Festival of Flowers. This is a huge festival that takes place in Medellin. We missed it because we had gone to Ecuador. Missing this was a tender spot in our relationship. I asked about the dates when buying the airlines tickets, but Diana did not recall. I did get to see the beautiful flowers anyway. There were commercial floral displays, with the companies large logos, and there were the smaller personal displays made by individuals. Each arrangement is judged.

The tradition is brought down from the history of the Spaniards being carried on the backs of the original Colombians. The Spaniards employed, or enslaved servants to be more accurate, to carry them through the land, a kind of taxi, if you will. On the backs of the poor the rich would be carried on chairs. The small chairs became the flower displays of today. Therefore, the parade is thousands of people carrying these flower arrangements on their back through the streets. This is something like the Parade of Roses in Los Angels every New Year's day. The displays are all natural, flower, or organic. Some are round, others square, but in a size that is large enough to be carried on the back. I got to see my festival in absence. The flowers were a little wilted, but the colors and arrangements were a wonderful eyeful.

When we entered the commercial center, the first shop was an open-air meat store. Big slabs of fresh meat were hanging on hooks. I laugh at my North American perceptions of things. The commercial center was a building with stalls of fruits and vegetables, and the meat shops, but not much more. One little shop sold commercial goods. Tuto bought a comb. The man tried to sell me something, but I declined. I took some photographs and we left.

We went down the second floor on a long steep ramp that stretched half the length of the building. I guess this was to roll the products up to the second floor on carts.

By the time we returned to the house, activity was taking place. Showers were being taken and the smell of cooked food was drifting through the front door. After breakfast, we went to the funeral home. The man who passed away is Auria's uncle. Auria is Diana's sister in law. The funeral home was a long, thin, large room with chairs lining the walls. Auria's mother sat with two other women saying a rosary and crying. The casket was a few feet away. I went up to see a dead man I had never laid eyes on before, said a prayer, and went back to sit with the others as they said the rosary in Spanish. Soon the rest of the family came by car with the flowers from the quinceanera the night before. I helped bring in the flowers from the street. In a Hollywood moment, I placed a group of flowers on the top of the casket and caused the lid to slam shut with a loud noise.

As we sat there, I saw many people come into the funeral home, go up to the open casket, pay their respects, and leave without even acknowledging the family. I asked Diana about this. It is the custom to come and pray for the deceased. Not saying anything to the family would be considered rude in North America, but here it was common. To go into a funeral home of someone you did not know would also be considered strange. Some of the viewers were barefoot farmers from the countryside. An array of people came in said a prayer and left within a few minutes.

The rest of the day we walked the little town, ate lunch, and I took a nap. I could not sleep, so I listened to my iPod in the children's bedroom. I just needed to be alone. I can take just so much time with anyone and I need to get to a place where I can sit, or lay, and be alone. I returned to the flower display at the commercial center with Diana after a brief return visit to the funeral home. The line of visitors was still filing through. The funeral mass was at four o'clock. I did not feel like sitting in the funeral home. We had a nice little walk. By this time I had not been alone with Diana for days.

At the funeral mass, the various family members were seated on each sides, or scattered in many locations around the church. Only the immediate family sat in the third row. The pallbearers were hired from the funeral home. Six males rolled the casket into the church and three females carried flowers. They all wore matching brown blazers and dark pants. The mass was long. There was an enormous amount of incense burning and I almost chocked from it. As the priest walked down the center isle, an echo of coughing people followed, myself included. My flu was rearing it's beastly head and the smoke added to my headache. At the end of the mass a group gathered at the front door of the church as the last prayers were said over the body. We stood off to one side with the family. There was a strange disconnect to the whole event for me. The church was filled with people who did not know the dead man. The funeral was dovetailed into a regularly scheduled mass. The sheer number of churchgoers made the mass seem impersonal and confusing. I do not know what happened at the cemetery, or if anyone went to the cemetery. The man had died from gangrene. His lower leg was removed but he died three days later from infection in the hospital. We left after saying goodbye to the mourning family members that stood in a huddle at the front of the church. People filed by without looking at them or the casket. We went walking in the tiny streets back to the house. We loaded the car and soon were on our way to the finca. Diana's uncle, aunt, nephew, the two of us, and the brother of Diana's sister in law (Albeiro) all climbed into a red jeep.

Entry Two: The day we left for here (San Pedro), we woke in the morning at Albeiro's house. We left the uncles funeral at four in Guarne the day before. We had to re-enter Medellin for a major road that lead north along the river valley at the base of an opposite mountain range. I was delighted to see hundreds of kites being flown. As we would rise or descend along the hilly route, the kites would be at eye level, or even far above our jeep. At one park alone, there were hundreds of kites. We assumed it was a kite festival.

I remember my visit to Bali. It was so nice to see the sky dotted with colorful kites of every shape. To me this represents the ultimate freedom. From as early as I remember, I had kites and to this day keep a few in the car. To stop and fly a kite is an exercise in self-awareness. A kite knows when the flyer is awake or when he is not paying attention. To lie on your back and gaze into the heavens is a pause in the day that nourishes the soul. One time when I was young in Southern California, I did an experiment. I secured the kite to a tree at sunset. Silly me, I assumed it would be there in the morning, flying, waiting to greet me. However, no, the winds had died in the night and my kite was blocks away, across the wide schoolyard with an endless white strand of hope. I learned to know the weather better. Recently I was appalled when Diana and I were stopped from flying a kite at the beach near our house. When I asked if I could move to a far away part of the beach where there were no people (which was the case anyway), I was told no. "The kite might hit someone on the beach or in the water." It is a sad day when so much energy goes into restricting such a leisurely pastime. This is one reason I want to leave the USA eventually. The insanity of over-legislating when common sense can be used is very troubling to me.

As we drove towards the finca, the road along the river that runs through Medellin eventually climbed higher and higher into the mountains. The buses and motorcycles sped along as if there were no centerline for traffic. They drove as if they were on flat ground, not a mountain highway. The views were spectacular. I had never driven on such high mountain roads and seen such gigantic breadth between valleys. I have been in the Rocky and Sierra Mountain ranges of North America, but the Colombian mountains dwarf these ranges. I am also accustomed to seeing pine trees in these high mountains, but in Colombia the terrain has trees and bushes that are tropical. Fabio also drove our jeep like a race-car driver. The double yellow (no passing) line meant nothing. If a motorcycle was coming and we were passing, it was inferred that the motorbike must move out of the way. Size determined right of way. The potholes in the road added an extra level of anxiety as we dodged death and passed anything that moved one second slower than us, even if it were on a curve, a blind curve, bus or no bus. All the while, the road was climbing in altitude as well as my fear. Couple my fear of heights with my fear of maniac drivers and there was some real high blood pressure at work.

We stopped for a rest and had some arepas at a truck stop. The waitress was very pleasant and the entire crowd was glued to a soccer match on TV's suspended from the ceiling. We later ascertained that the waitress passed me some fake money. It was dusk as we began to move inland away from the valleys' edge, into rain, and rolling hills (more like rolling mountains, but rolling). By now, the drive was becoming dangerous even for Fabio. With nightfall and a driving rain, and the inside window fogging up, Uncle Fabio suggested we spend the night at Albeiro's. There was good reason considering the only visible guide was an occasional reflector on the roadside, no street lights, and pitch black visibility.

Albeiro manages a small grocery store, so we stopped there in the town of Santa Rosa. This town is where Diana's mother grew up. We passed the lot where the family home had stood, now replaced by a small store. We got into the heart of Santa Rosa and parked the jeep. I was stunned by the number of youths in the street. It was a Friday night and the tiny street was filled with kids and teenagers. We went into the grocery store. Albeiro took care of the store closing, and called several people for the next days opening. Next, we set off for his apartment.

One curious aspect of traveling with others and in a foreign country is that people do not necessarily make a point to communicate the details of what plans are in motion. They assume I understand Spanish and follow every conversation, when I do not. I thought Albeiro was going to the finca with us. No, he was going to Santa Rosa only. He had come to Guarne for the quinceanera two days before. The unexpected funeral of the uncle caused him to miss a day's work, so he was only being dropped off, and we were to continue on to the finca. The point I am trying to make is that I operate my life in a way that I like to know what is going on. Here, yes, I am literally along for the ride, but I still want to know the plan. More than once the "plan" has not turned out to be the "plan" at all, because I have do not a full understanding of Spanish. I try to back track in my memory to the moment the misunderstanding began. This is something I do in most relationships anyway. I want to know where and when my interpretations differed from the other person. This happens in life all the time. To me it is a peculiar detail when this deconstruction takes place. I do not do this to blame, but to figure out why there was a misunderstanding, and when the split of minds occurred. In a marriage, this may or may not be the solution of differences, but it helps to be aware of how different we all are when creating a shared reality.

Albeiro took us down some hills to a tiny street into a nice clean, new apartment. The house was freezing to me. No one else seemed to pay any attention. I had been nursing the flu (gripa in Spanish) for a few days, following its progression from my sinuses, to my throat, to my bronchial, and then to my lungs. I was coughing every few minutes. This started at Mark's house in Bogotá two weeks earlier, healed somewhat in Ecuador, and then returned in a kinder gentler flu this time. In Ecuador, I bought antibiotics to knock it out, but the cold weather and change in locations never allowed my body to heal totally while traveling. This seems to happen to me every time I go south of the Equator. My body must know my meridians are all switched around, not to mention I am usually south in their winter, which is our summer (North America).

We ate some sandwiches, bundled up, and went to see the little town. As the walk began, I noticed more kids playing in the streets, completely unsupervised. Here it is long past darkness and the streets are crawling with youth. We climbed a long steep stairway, turned a corner, and found ourselves in an ally full of tents with vendors. I thought this was a nice touch for a small town on a Friday night. When we exited the ally, we entered a plaza filled with hundreds of people wearing Colombian "cowboy" hats and ponchos. They were all in a very festive mood. There were actually thousands of people. This was no typical Friday night. The plaza had a huge stage with dancers and a live loud band playing. There was lots of food and alcohol being served all around the parameter of the central square. After asking, I was told this was the town's annual birthday celebration. This explained why so many people were in the street when we first got to the store, but I was still struck by the number of young people. It is not that the old are kept away; they were there too. It is that every two adults have produced at least eight to ten children. This has gone on for a number of generations and now the result is a staggering number of young kids. No birth control and a strong Catholic ethic, lead to a population explosion, something not so apparent in the USA.

We listened to the music of "Banana". There were two female dancers that must lubricate their bone joints because I have never seen such gyrations of hip and arm movements. The plaza was full of dancers, couples embracing, drunks, lovers, hats, ponchos, and sheer fun taking place. On top of this people looked at me like I was E.T. I know I was the only Gringo for miles and years. We wandered back to the apartment, where we closed the night on single beds with one blanket each. Diana and Sebastian shared a bed, head to feet, on the floor. I slept in a tiny single bed. The room was so small with the two beds that there was no place to walk. In the middle of the night, I stepped on one body when I got up to pee.

The next morning I went out for a few photographs and returned in time for breakfast and our good byes to Albeiro. He is a devout Catholic and played all the music for his uncle's funeral. He plays music by ear, like me. He is a bigger than usual Colombian with a large nose which makes his singing voice strong and deep. He strikes me as the forty-year-old virgin. His house has two reproduced art works, one of a Rembrandt ("The Periodical Son"), the other a large portrait of Christ, This is in his bedroom. Like so many people here, he is a good person. He is easy to be with and his kindness comes across. He prays a lot, enjoys family, and treats others with respect. Where are all the "bad people" here? In Long Island on my daily drive to work, I see at least one a--hole that drives like the world owes him, or her, a favor. Rudeness on the road is so common in New York that it is expected as part of life. Here the people are unusually good toward strangers. How refreshing.

Third Entry: I will continue writing about our current location and how we got here at the finca in San Pedro de Los Milagros. This is a small "farm" owned by the uncle who lives in Queens, New York, near us on Long Island. We got here this morning after a drive through a couple of small towns. The road seemed to wander along the top of the world. We could tell we were on a high plateau with an occasional long view, far off hills and green forests. One of the towns was San Pedro. To my surprise, we saw some of the most beautiful religious art I had ever seen. The basilica in this small town is huge and has a series of ceiling painting that are outstanding. These paintings are very realistic. They follow the life story of Christ and Old Testament Stories. The art was painted on canvases hanging flat directly above our heads. I guess the art was created in the nineteen fifties. The book explaining the art was in Spanish, and the book did not have any reproductions. I found this strange. The paintings are at least twenty feet in length, but way up in the ceiling of the basilica. They were breathtaking. One impression that stuck with me was that Christ was smiling in several of the paintings. Not the crucifixion, but the resurrection, yes. The artist had painted a Christ that looked human with emotions and smiles.

The Pope is visiting the basilica next year, so there is a renovation taking place of the church and accompanying town square. In fact, the square was nothing more than a pile of dirt with the beginnings of concrete walkways. The tall, green plastic drapery around the town center made it seem a bit strange. The walks and fountain were only visible from the steps of the basilica, above street level.

When we arrived at the finca, Tuto was already there fixing his white Fiat with one of millions of problems. He and Morelia had come in a separate car that morning. He keeps a set of tools in the trunk. The car is a never-ending project. It was broke before we went to Ecuador, but he and Diana's mother picked us up in the car on our return. This time the car had a problem with the plastic bumper because it had rattled loose on the road to the finca. Tuto was fixing the car and Morelia was cooking. In Colombia, the oldest woman is always in charge of the kitchen and cooking. The rest of us do the eating.

We spent a little time rearranging our luggage so Tuto and Morelia could take the suitcase back for us. I stupidly brought one large suitcase, a heavy burden that would have been double hell on the small bus that will take us back to Medellin on Wednesday. We have lugged the thing around a couple of days already. I insisted on bringing it because I have the computer and the cameras inside. I still have them. Everything will go into one bag for the crowded small bus. All I really need is a change of clothes, but the computer and cameras are not to be parted with. I did not bring the computer to Ecuador and missed writing so many details, which I will attempt to remember later.

Tuto fixed the problem with his car, I began a new painting, we ate lunch, and I organized the suitcase for Tuto to take back. Sebastian, Diana's nephew, started a painting too. We are painting the finca. I will leave it as a gift for Diana's uncle. People love paintings of their houses. We had a great lunch of rice, beans, chicken sausage, and good company. I stop myself every so often and remind myself to look at the love and kindness present in these people. Not once have I heard anyone be ugly to anyone else. They say how important the family is and have the loving bonds so many people in the world need. I do not think they take it for granted, or make much of a conscious effort to promote "family values". They just have them. Period.

I do not know if there is a dangerous demon hiding some where in the family, telling them to be civil for the moment, or if this is so real that, there is nothing to fight about. The level of respect is a natural fact; no one is sitting around saying, "aren't we great". The children behave very well, and any member of the family gives the occasional correction to the children. No one is trying to impress anyone else or talking about someone else. The major function is to be good to each other without it being stated as a need. I am astounded by the simplicity and manors of this family. I am very lucky.

After Tuto and Morelia left for Medellin with Sebastian, we sat and talked on the front porch with Piedad and Fabio. They would stay an extra day with us. We drank beer and talked about a friend of Diana's who married for the papers in the States and is being blackmailed by the man who married her. The whole thing is beyond my comprehension because the woman is afraid of a man who is guilty of lying to immigration officials. He continues to extort money from her. Diana's friend fears the man who she married will turn her in. He has broken the law, just like her. He threatens to report her to immigration for a fraud he also committed. To make matters worse her lawyer tells her to pay the man. Not all the pieces fit for me, but it sounds like the lawyer has his finger in the pie with the man who married Diana's friend. I cannot believe the stupidity of this whole situation. There are millions of snakes in the jungle, if you pick one up you will be bitten. I get very upset and angry whenever I hear an update of this story.

The finca is a fairyland house. It has a red roof, red trim, and white walls with lots and lots of flowers. The house feels like dwarfs and elves should be running around. The low eves and tiny stairs are not built for a six-foot tall man like me. I am here only two days and I want to stay here the rest of our time in Colombia, which is three days. However, Diana has many things to do. One errand is to revisit the tattoo/ beauty salon and have one eyeliner re-darkened. I think I will pass the joy of this event. However, we have to return to Medellin. We do this by bus tomorrow. We have been watching to see what the times the bus goes by here. The road is so bad it is a wonder that a motorcycle can pass, not to mention a big bus. So far, the bus has gone by at eleven and two. It goes up the dead end valley and returns about forty-five minutes later. We know the bus is coming because the driver beeps his horn as he slowly passes each house.

The ground floor of the finca is red brick. The interior has all natural wood; this gives the darkness in the house a feeling of warmth. Upstairs it is always warmer because heat rises and the red roofing shingles collect warmth. The rooms are so small that our split-level-bed kept the door from opening; below my bed, a second bed pulls out. All the floors upstairs are wooden and creek whenever we move in bed or while walking. It dawned on me last night I have not spent one single minute alone with my wife in three days. We slept on a pull out bed in Guarne the night of the quinceanera. We slept in separate beds in Santa Rosa. Here in the finca the walls are paper thin, we can hear Fabio snoring like he is in bed with us.

When I was a child in California, we had an "A" frame cabin, just like the finca. There is even a spiral staircase like we had. Therefore, this place is double magic to me. The flowers everywhere and the bright colors make me happy. There is a large patio out front and a wrap-around porch with the typical Colombian rocking chairs. There are hanging plants on the front porch like every house in Colombia. The house itself has tiny rooms upstairs and three bathrooms. I am like Gandalf here. I hit my head every time I pass through the front door. My head has a red bloody spot to prove my height. When I use the toilet upstairs, my knees touch the wall. I have to stoop down when ever I pass through all the doors. In the photographs we take, I am at least one head length above all the Colombians. Diana comes up to my shoulders. These people are small. I just wish they made doors taller.

We returned to Medellin by bus and took a cab to Diana's parent's apartment building. When I went to pay the taxi driver, he insisted the money was fake. I did not believe him. I handed him another bill and his reaction was twice as angry. The third bill was too large so Diana took the bills to a corner store to get change. She returned and sure enough, the two bills were counterfeits. The third larger bill was real and we paid the taxi driver with the change made at the corner store. That night we showed Fabio the bills and he explained to me how to identify counterfeit bills. The Colombians check their money every time they are handed change. I have seen this but never knew why. The thickness of the bill was wrong; it indeed felt like regular paper. The watermarks were blurry, and the metallic strand that runs up and down the bill was not present. The only place I used my money was in the restaurant days before. The other times I used coins from my pocket.

The last few days we packed and did as much of nothing as possible. Tuto took us to the airport in the morning and we left for the last leg of our summer, Panama. We had one bag each. It was a very short flight. Now I could be alone with my wife again. Had the family not been so pleasant to be around I might have felt like leaving earlier. My own family could never have been so well behaved and harmonious. I knew I would miss each and every one of my new Colombian family.

Chapter 14. Panama.

Day One: We are in Panama. I lived here fifty-three years ago. My earliest memories are of hot sand on the beach, me crying from my feet getting burned on the sand, the temperature, and being whipped for going into the jungle. I was in the jungle with my sister and brother. Just a few feet inside the jungle, the insects amazed us. The colors and amount of insects were breathtaking to me. I remember looking at the insects like they were creatures from a far off universe. I thought they were communicating with me. They swarmed within inches of my face and feet, yet I had no fear of them. I was mesmerized by their patterned colors. I was four years old. As I reflect back, the worst part of this beautiful experience was the drastically contrasting event that soon followed. It was my first memory of many, being whipped with a belt by my father. He found by using a strong whistling, which he did all my life. The whistle always symbolized terror and the authority of his belt. Years later, I finally stole the belt and he never found it again. I learned how to keep a secret to myself.

Today I am sitting on a balcony on the forth floor of a luxury apartment. We are "staying with friends", a site I found on the Internet. The elderly couple that greeted us last night are wonderful. The apartment is inside their house and has much more than we expected. It has a big bathroom, TV, big bed, and lots of closets. It is a large room with marble floors. After our last hotel in Ecuador, it is quite a change. The room is huge with excellent accommodations.

The owners are Panamanian. They are in their late sixties and are very nice. It is like staying with family. Diana had a tough day yesterday leaving her parents house. She cried several times. She loves her family, especially her father, and the City of Medellin. I know I cannot fill that void. I know we need a lot more time to create the bond between us that she has with her close family. I have confidence this will happen. I just hope she can hold on long enough for all her dreams to come true. The couple here in the apartment are comforting to her, like her parents.

The night before our departure Diana's mother was asking me about leaving, if I was glad to be going home. I said yes. I miss my home when I am away so long. I see Panama as a kind of stepping-stone back into New York for Diana. We have one week before we go, and one week in a place that is similar to Costa Rica and Colombia, only really more like Miami in the tropics. However, more importantly it will be a transition returning to our new marriage and away from life in the past. We need to reconnect and have the focus on our time together. It is extremely modern here.

Diana loves her city life back in Medellin. I am a country boy at heart. Cities are too overwhelming to me. Where we live in New York is like the country, as far as it is not populated. It is quiet, close to the beach and the salt-water marshes. In Medellin, the traffic and people make it a bustling place. Also in Medellin, we instantly step into a life that is filled with people in her neighborhood. Every body knows every body. The man, Ricardo, and his down-syndrome son, who sits at the corner in a wheelchair, watches the neighborhood, and sees exactly who is coming and going. (Ricardo was shot by a drug dealer in the time of Pablo Escobar.) The woman who sits in the sun on the street every morning cleaning her baby, knows who passes. The beautician around the corner knows all the local gossip. Diana had years of being in one place. I have moved so many times I cannot keep track. However, my heart goes out to Diana for leaving and coming to be with me. Today she said she was torn because she loves her family. I know she does not really like New York.

I have opened up my home thinking it was paradise because of the location and being so quiet. Yet to my wife the isolation is boring, and the quiet is worse. The contrast between the two countries is so dramatic it is clear to see. The people in Colombia have each other. In the USA, we have our property and things that keep us occupied and isolated. I did not say happy. Many of the things I have disagreed with about my country are the same things that are very obvious to an outsider. However, what am I to do? I cannot change where I live. Diana and I had a discussion in the morning as we walked along the streets before leaving Medellin. The pressure on me for Diana to be happy is tremendously difficult. I got a little miffed at hearing that New York is this hell I was bringing my wife back to. I was telling Diana about how I have worked so hard to get where I am, and that she will have to also. Getting a car and becoming less dependent on me will resolve her immediate "problem". However, life is hard no matter where you live. I am the bad guy even though I have shared everything and spent hours driving her back and forth to classes. I call her life with me a "project" because I have been working in her behalf for the entire year, from helping her get a job to filing immigration papers. Most men get married and the "project" is not there; the women come in as a full partner and they have an economic union that reinforces one and another. Sometimes I feel as if I am raising a child because I am paying attention to her needs and leaving mine aside.

This is different than most modern marriages in that she totally depends on me economically and emotionally. It is different and this is what makes it special to me. I am making a big investment for the future and know exactly what we are building. When Diana finishes school, she will be independent and have more than she will need. She will be in a position to share with me.

Right now, I am paying for everything. The future will be more balanced economically.

I look at things like this. I could not find the kind of family values, good moral character, and especially the non-materialistic woman I wanted, in New York. Maybe this is a self-inflicted myth but I went out of my country and sought a woman that fit my dreams. Seeking an outsider has produced unseen difficulties. At the same time, we have created a very different type of relationship than most. The blessing and the curse of what we wanted, and what we got, is all part of life. Life is never easy and always challenging. I can deal with it. I am settled enough, old enough, and have enough money to feel secure in my insecurities. Our age difference of twenty years gives me an unusual perspective on life. I see a bigger picture than Diana. That is ok because she adds many things to the picture that are more important than the big picture.

She is like I once was. She is living through a great transition. I am attracted to her friendly loving ways. This makes me very happy. The childish aspect of her personality, that is impulsive with money and overly sensitive to criticisms, is difficult. One of the big issues in Colombia was her wanting to "bail out" her father from money problems. More than once I told her that she should not be giving large sums of money to her father. More importantly that she needed the money for herself. I am really trying to wean her off the parental guilt. We have funds that are for "our" time together and I do not feel bad for keeping a boundary in place.

She provided much economic support to her parents because she lived with them until the age of thirty-five. Now her father was asking her for money because of his problems with the car. The car was broken down, and her father caused an accident in the building where they live. The subsequent construction and repairs were large amounts of money. I got cold hearted and told her it was not her problem. "But I love my father". Yes, I know she does. However, I see a pattern of her saving him from himself, when it is better to let her separate from that kind of interaction. I do not understand that kind of entanglement with my parents. I do not really know the answer.

In a somewhat ironic twist, her bank-card did not work here in Panama or Colombia. She had very little money, but it was hers. Because of the bank-card not working, I had full control of the money and had to give her money from her account. (I can move money on line from one account to another. In Costa Rica, she could withdraw from her account, but in Colombia, she was declined. We will find out why when we return.) I love Diana's father. He is a kind and wonderful man, but I do not like him asking her for help when she should be focusing on her future, and her life, and her independence. We are well off compared to the Colombia standard of living, but the emotional aspect of a father daughter relationship (to me anyway), should be where the father is a provider not the daughter. Now I am being a real jerk. However, the "cultural" aspect of Diana providing for the aging parents is another big difference that rubs me wrong. In the third world, the children help the parents; in the USA, the parents are perpetually helping their children. I see this as being resolved when Diana has her career and what she does with her money is her business. Now I am providing the economic support so I feel the focus should be on her long-term future, not the parent's immediate needs. I am playing the role of parent with Diana. This is thin ice on a thawing situation that will change with time, or heat up and melt into anger. Everybody needs to be patient.

We all talked one night about buying a finca (farm) and having her parents live in a separate house, or apartment. We all agreed this will happen after the most important thing in Diana's life is completed, her education. Therefore, they understand where I am heading with my dreams, yet in the mean time I feel a bit guilty for being the one withholding funds. I am looking at a bigger picture that will have everyone in it. The same goes with having a child. I do not want to be the sole provider. If we have a child now, I will be the one giving total economic support. I do not feel that is correct. The woman should share in the economic responsibility. In turn, I should share with the raising of a child, emotionally and spiritually. My mother did not "work" (ha, ha. She worked like a slave.), but my father did not really share with the raising of the children. He was the authority and disciplinarian, my mother suffered because of this set up. I do not want to repeat their sins. I have to balance how I see the right or wrong in what a relationship should be. Because my parents life was so screwed up, it took me years to realize how screwed up I was as a product of their dysfunction. The American dream is full of curses that absolutely need to be rethought and changed.

I have been writing and sitting on a porch in Panama City, listening to the tropical birds, and Diana just came out and said good morning. She has little idea of how much I care about her and love her. I tell her so, but I know she does not know the positive affect she has had on my life. She is an angel in my life and gives me great purpose and hope.

Day 2: We found this spacious apartment on the Internet, like so many other things in our life. The elderly couple are consistently very nice. The woman, Cecelia, took to Diana immediately. One of the things I love about Diana is the way she loves people and opens up to them. People love the attention and she is good at showing them instant respect and companionship. They rattle off the Spanish faster than I can follow. Sisters they are indeed. Mario is the husband. He has a ponytail, like me, and speaks a little English. I am not sure what he did, but from the looks of the apartment, he had a good profession. We are on the fourth floor in the middle of the city. It is near anything we want. The balcony is especially nice. It is where I sit and write in a big stuffed reclining chair.

Cecelia called a taxi service. She told us it was cheaper and better to hire a taxi by the hour instead of going on the city tours in a bus with a bunch of people. So we spend fifty dollars and begin at ten in the morning.

We started the day by walking across the street and shopping for food. The apartment has a small refrigerator and we filled it with juices, yogurt, fruit, and some sandwich supplies. The market was expensive, but close. We got a weeks supply of breakfasts and lunches. The people who own the market are Chinese and spoke Spanish. I was tripping on them because my thoughts were that they would never live in New York City speaking Spanish. I spoke in Spanish and felt like I was communicating better with them than if I was in New York City because the Chinese there usually speak very little English, or just enough to hand you your change. (This is my narrow-minded ethnocentric side, which is tainted by my white middle class life.) I enjoyed this new type of encounter with the Chinese people.

I wonder many times where my perceptions of people come from and why they stick to me so much. I work in a multicultural environment, yet I often catch myself thinking in such strange "white" terms. I have come to the conclusion that the imprinting my father did on me was very profound and takes a life time to break out of. My father was a tolerant racist. He believed that all people were good, with some bad elements, but he never mixed with people other than whites. Later on in his life, he had some neighbors and friends that were of different races, but he did not believe that anyone should marry out of their race. "Life would be too hard for the children". His view of gays were that they were sick and to be feared. Those shadows stay with a child and linger into adulthood. I also wonder why I predict how backwards a country is going to be. When I arrive in a country I am always saying to myself how modern it is and how the people are just like back home in New York. I have some preconceived images that nothing is as good as the good ol' USA. This is total nonsense. Life is life, different, but people have TVs, cars, and houses, eat food, and have all the same emotions. In foreign countries roads are just not as smooth and the cracks in the sidewalk are acceptable.

After breakfast and a chat with Cecelia we were off in a taxi to the Panama Canal. I lived here fifty-two years ago. I saw some old military housing that looked familiar, but who knows where I lived back then. The canal was very interesting. The taxi driver, a black Panamanian man with a gold front tooth named Oscar, was very good as a tour guide. We paid the eight dollars each to enter the canal, saw a movie explaining the history, watched the boats in the hydraulic locks, and visited the four floors of museum. The observation deck was a great place to see the movement of ships right up close. Diana was raptured by the experience. She would yell, "Papi, Papi. Look at they tug boats. Look at they water and the gates". We had fun.

The taxi driver took us on a long drive past the bridge that crosses the canal to a thin raised road that goes way out in the water. This was where General Noriega had his private home. The disappointment of this area was that it could have been in Miami or California. The same chain of restaurants in every city across the USA was there. Along the ride we could see all the huge ships with tons and tons of cargo. Who is buying all this stuff and who is going to fill the landfills with the trash? I am worried at the pace of consumerism and what is really happening to the planet.

The next phase of our tour was sad. We left the modern commercial zone and passed through the poorest barrios into the historic old town. This area reminded me of the Philippines. People hung out of windows and doors. Clothes lines were strewn across buildings and ally ways in an abstract design that contributed to the visible hardship on the faces of the poor. I had the camera going, but knew using it was an invasion of hardship. The taxi insulated us by the quick ride through, but my heart was feeling sad. Soon we came to the tourist places and the historic old buildings. The shops were beyond our budget. There were no bargains to be had. A strange dichotomy between what we had seen less than a mile away and the clean empty shopping street did not make the browsing any fun.

A few blocks away we walked past some monuments to the Spaniards, up some stairs to an open street that went the length of the waters edge. Three hundred degrees of water surrounded us. Some Indians were selling fabrics and I bought a few things. The negotiations were tougher than in Ecuador. These people did not budge. They have their price set and they all worked together on keeping the price. I know how to bargain. I am not weak when it comes to the art of negotiation. We bought some beautiful handcrafts.

The driver took us to another set of historic buildings that looked like a small community, or settlement. The church was well persevered and the surrounding buildings all had nicely painted tropical wood eves with ornate cutout designs. The buildings looked Dutch because of the square, not round or curved appearances. A man played a banjo and his soft music followed us in and out of the tourist shops. There we bought more from the Indians in the shops.

The following attraction was where we spent the most time, well over two hours. Our taxi driver, Oscar, was hungry and we ordered some chicken empanadas. When we arrived there were a dozen children on the steps of a small white Spanish style church doing traditional folk dances. Each pair of male, female dancers wore traditional Panamanian cloths. The girls wore long white lacy dresses with shawls, all in white. The boys had shirts with pleated front panels and round hats that folded back in the front. Their clothes were designed for the heat. It was wonderful to see them, so serious, all smiles, but well choreographed. They twirled and stepped their way for more than an hour. We ordered the food, which took at least forty-five minutes. The check came in three minutes.

At one point the dancers came into the small audience and gathered partners. I was chosen to be the partner of a young girl about twelve years old. She was delicate and wore a floor length, white pleated skirt with a blouse of white lace. Her hair was jet black, pulled back, and had decorative white brooches pinned into each side of her hair. These brooches looked like they had their origins in Spain. The dancing was simple and easy to follow. She gently guided me and smiled the whole while.

I once did a similar group dance in China at a culture park. I was invited to join the group and dance in a big circle. The outcome was very comic. This was around eight years ago and I was on a one day trip into Mainland China from Hong Kong. I had a pair of baggy pants that were way too big for me. I was pulled out of the audience to come and take part in the dance. As I spun in the circle my pants dropped past me knees. I am frantically grasping at them, pulling them up, and at the same time trying to keep in step with the rest of the dancers in the circle. Up and back down my trousers slipped whenever I let go of them to take the dancer next to me by the hand. The crowd of people in the seats was hysterically laughing at me. I needed a belt. I bowed to the audience at the end of this funny dance. They gave me a big round of applause. As I danced with this young girl I was secretly checking my pants to make sure they would not slip.

We finished the small lunch, which was meant to be a snack because we had food waiting back at the apartment. Oscar took us to the center of the city, near where we are staying, and showed us the local Internet and food stores. We paid him, said our thanks, came up stairs to make lunch and have a nap. We also went to an ATM machine and took out more money before returning.

In the afternoon we walked to an Internet café where Diana called her mother. I went on the computer, but had a hard time figuring out the complicated system to log on. I was handed a slip of paper with a bunch of numbers. I had to ask for help several times as Diana talked to her mom. We ended the day at mass. As we walked out the church and crossed the street we were startled by the sound of screeching tires. We were a few feet away from a near accident and could have well been the victims of the wild traffic here. Diana related our miraculous save to the importance of having gone to mass and prayed in thanks.

Day four: Tomorrow we take the bus to the City of Colon on the Caribbean side of this slender land mass. We may stay in a hotel, or come back on the bus the same day. We do not know. Yesterday we did a few sight seeing jaunts here in the city. We waited on the pounding rain that was so bad it stopped all traffic. After the rain, around ten o'clock, we went to a shopping mall. I hate shopping malls but did this for Diana. We found a very good bargain on a Nativity scene for ten dollars in one of the department stores. It was made in China. The rain slowed more and we began to walk up into the newer more modern part of the city. More rain and a lack of enthusiasm because of the heat turned us back around seeking shelter in the mall once again. We came back to the apartment with our package and ate lunch.

Mario told us about an art exhibition right near us, so we went off looking for it, but never found it. Instead, we hired a taxi for two hours and went back to the old town where we had seen many interesting buildings. We visited the Alter of Gold. This is a church where the local people tricked the pirate, Captain Morgan. They had painted all the gold with black charcoal. When Morgan saw the altar he thought the church needed money so he gave a donation. We saw the altar, a tall spectacular work of art covered in gold leaf. It was nice, but our visit to Quito took the "ah" out of the churches here. We then returned to the lookout point where the modern city was visible from the street that ran along the waters edge. The same Indians were selling just like the day before. We had a newer, nicer taxi this time. The driver, named Gustavo, accommodated us for ten dollars an hour, and kept our fee time right on the mark. We went across the bridge of the "Americas" to a park where sleepy fisherman leaned over bridges and swimmers laughed with each other in a small lagoon. I took pictures. Gustavo was married with two children. He showed us a card that said he was an ordained minister and played religious songs in the taxis' disk player. As we looked at the altar of gold, he and I agreed it had little to do with the message of Christ.

I bought another "malla" (as they call them) from an Indian man. This is the hand-sewn tapestry on a black background. Brightly colored strips of cloth are cut into many pieces and puzzled together to create an animal, usually a jungle animal. He seemed to know I would not pay what he asked and came down in price right away. I usually buy things in pairs, so I bought another. Afterwards, the taxi dropped us off in the center of the city. We went to dinner in a Colombian restaurant and ordered arepas with chicken. We also had some fried plantain and yucca, fried like a French fried potato. We wanted to walk off the dinner in our stomachs, so we went looking for a park Mario had told us about. We got lost, but in a good way. When we finally found the park it was a big let down. It was a playground with a few trees, lots of people, and very small. There was a group of young people with their music blasting. They were going into wild hand and arm gyrations in time with the music. I think they were a dance team rehearsing for a music video. It took us an hour to find the park and three minutes to walk through and leave for home.

We knew we had to rise early to get to the bus, so we watched a little TV, and then went to sleep by nine. This night we did not use the air conditioner, just an electric fan. We slept much better. In the morning the sun was shinning on one half of the sky, but the clouds were rolling in fast. It looked like it could rain half the day again. We will go by taxi and then by bus to Colon.

Day six: Yesterday it was very interesting to see the City of Colon. We started early with a taxi ride to the National Bus Terminal. By 9:30 we were on the road in an air-conditioned bus with a movie playing. The bus was dark when we entered; the curtains were drawn to keep the heat out and the TV screen visible. The bus was running in the terminal to keep the air conditioning going. The terminal was filled with hundreds of brightly colored buses parked in long organized rows. After pulling out of the terminal we passed through several tolls, three within the first twenty minutes. In the center of the country there were some tiny towns, but for most of the route there were few houses or businesses. This was the central rain forests. The further east we went it became more populated, and poorer. We entered the first major intersection outside Colon and the police stood under a bridge wearing heavy vests with large firearms. There were at least seven of them in the shade at one makeshift post.

As the bus entered the town it was obvious the population was mostly black and very poor. The bus driver announced the duty free zone and most of the people exited the bus. We also exited the bus and walked a few blocks to a McDonalds. We used the restrooms, ate our own tuna fish sandwiches, and bought a Sundae. One thing I noticed that struck me as unusual was that two young men had cut into the line and went to the counter. The manager, a woman, told them they would have to return to the back of the line. However, she also told them they needed to show respect for the others who were in line before them. This impressed me because in the USA such a public correction of behavior would seldom take place. We seem to tolerate rude behavior in the States and not address the most important ingredient, respect and why it is needed. Teaching seldom takes place in public places, when it is so appropriate and needed.

The heat and visible desperation of those on the street pushed us further toward the duty free zone. We entered the first street of what was a walled area. A man in a uniform stopped us and asked us for our papers. "What papers?", I asked. We had to go to an office and get entry papers. Therefore, we walked another block. Inside an office there were men sitting in rows of chairs waiting behind windows at counters. We were directed to a window. The woman asked us for our tourist paper and passports. We had the tourist papers, but the passports were back at the apartment. With a little convincing and some honesty we were soon inside the zone. I did have a photocopy of my passport and drivers license, but Diana had only the tourist card. All tourists are issued a special paper when they enter the country. By luck I had brought these alone.

The duty free zone was one of the strangest places on earth I have ever been. Most of the shops had a sign on the door, "wholesalers only". Men in sunglasses walked around and approached us to take us to shops, but we wanted to see just for ourselves. These men were hawkers trying to make a buck. However, why? I guess they were guides. It was hot; there was not one tree, or green vegetation anywhere. The stores were expensive looking. Inside these air conditioned vaults sat beautiful receptionists wearing low cut blouses with lots of cleavage and tight dresses. Each building was very modern with much glass and shinny aluminum, but the streets were like a chapter out of Dante's Divine Comedy. They were bleak, lifeless, and baron. The wires running overhead looked like they would fall at any moment. They crisscrossed the streets in a weird hodgepodge of unplanned networking. The pavements were cracked with utility covers missing and deep dangerous holes waiting to break an unsuspecting ankle. It was a concrete hell and the heat was deadly. We walked on the shady side of the street just to keep cool. The air was as still as death.

This went on for about twenty blocks, or more. We walked in the zone for a few blocks. We went into maybe five stores because "only wholesalers were allowed" in the other ones. The first store was like a dollar store. Diana bought some things for her hair and an umbrella. We asked the stores people where we could find a hotel and a beach to swim. "No, only crocodiles and the canal".

The second store was more exciting. It was draperies and tablecloths. I have a thing for fabrics. Ever since I was young in Pakistan I love to look at fabrics and lace. This store was a gift to find. We spent seventy dollars on tablecloths and fabrics. The designs were very beautiful. There was one rack where every item was five dollars so we went wild. We bought gifts and one fabric for the house in Costa Rice where the color scheme is orange. Most of the embroidery was made in China, but we also bought a pretty fabric from India with embroidered gold lines and sequins. We briefly spoke to an Orthodox Jew from Israeli. I asked him if he was from New York. "No". He asked where we came from. "New York". It's funny but I fully expected him to be a New Yorker. He was with a man that kept pestering him to leave. This man was one of his tour guides in dark glasses. Why the time limitations? It all added up to a surreal, dream-like environment. I expected to see a watch dripping over a tree as in Salvador Dali's surreal artworks in this strange dry place.

The shops went on for ever as far as I could tell. I was getting buggy in such a stale environment. I am thinking to myself, "this is like the other side of the Berlin Wall"; only it is Capitalism being kept under guard. Men lurked on the streets and lines of people stood waiting for lunch with vendors on wheels who were cooking on the street. There were no restaurants. No place to go inside and buy a cold drink or water. The prices in the few stores we were allowed in were not much better than a discount department chain store. I really wanted to get out of there. It was the opposite of what I had imagined it to be.

We exited to a street outside the "wall". It looked dangerous. One man passing by warned us to get a taxi because we would be robbed with our shopping bags so visible. We soon climbed into a cab and a big warm booming voice said in clear English, "Where ya from?" Our driver was a retired army man. His name was Ellington. "People call me the Duke." "Where do you want to go?" We told him we heard about the Washington Hotel. "Ok daddy, but here's the thing around here. Be very careful. I tried to warn this dude from Australia, but he did not listen. They shot his hand. I told him not to wander these streets alone, but he didn't listen." Duke became our guardian angel. We asked him about a beach and hotel. "No hotels, no beach around here". However, he offered to take us to a nice beach with a restaurant; it was south about forty minutes away and twenty-five dollars for two hours with him waiting for the return trip. We took his offer.

I enjoyed this man. He had moved to Panama and married a Colombian woman. They have three children and nice house he built for ninety thousand dollars. He had been stationed in Vietnam and Germany. He was sixty-six years old. He had white hair, a white beard, and gold teeth in the front that contrasted with his dark black skin. His demeanor was very different from the typical Panamanian we had met. He told us he was from Texas, but had been raised in Panama by military parents who also moved there. He was proud of being an American, proud of his Colombian wife, and a very pleasant man to be with. He had an air of confidence and a beatnik voice that sounded like music and poetry. While taking us to the beach he even briefly stopped at the police station, gave them a wave hello, and drove on. I am not sure if this was for the police, or us, but they waved him on from a wide-open window.

We arrived at our beach after a ride though some beautiful countryside with green pastures speckled with white Brahma bulls. The beach was a piece of heaven after such a strange morning in the duty free zone. We had to go swimming. The water was clear turquoise blue, and calling us. We also put the tablecloths into the trunk of the taxi for sake keeping. We went into a changing room where we were charged twenty-five cents each, and exited onto the beach. I left the bag of cameras and money with Duke. Diana asked me about our valuables. I said we have to trust people. I handed him the bag in front of the two women who worked at the restaurant. Really there is no other way to get through traveling, or life. If we do not build trust with strangers we would never survive. The other side of this natural fear is the gift we give strangers by trusting them. I have never been burned doing what I do because I believe respect is the strongest power on earth.

We enjoyed the water for half an hour, and then I went back for the cameras and to order lunch. We walked along the beach where a two year old played in the water with his mother. The little boy saw us and ran to us. He handed me a small shell with an enthusiastic smile. I secretly said a prayer for him, wishing him all the luck and kindness a long life could bring. I shot photographs of the beautiful beach. Other young boys snorkeled in the shallow water with goggles on. They were looking for fish. The water was warm on the surface, getting progressively cooler as it deepened. However, it was the kind of cool water that refreshes. I know we will not be in warm water again until we return to Costa Rica in December. Lunch was ready right when the waitress said, "one half hour". It was rice with shredded cabbage, and a nice fried fish, head, eyes, fins and all. The cost, four dollars each. Maybe twice what the locals pay, but we are on vacation living the high life (on a budget).

The ride back to Colon with Duke was as entertaining and educational as the ride had been to the beach. Duke told us stories about his life, how he met his wife, and how he built his house with the help of his neighbors. The poverty got more prevalent as we entered the city. The duty free zone looked like an army camp from the main highway. The City of Colon is in bad shape. Once a building is built and painted, that is the last time it will ever be touched. Some of the buildings had not been painted for over one hundred years. Clothes lines and people hung from every balcony.

Duke warned us to be safe, show no money, and so we went straight from the taxi to the express bus. Again the bus was dark, air conditioned, and a movie was playing. While looking outside the bus, I watched a million things happening as daily life goes on every where; selling, running, laughing, screaming at taxis', shopping, gambling, hocking and getting to where ever one is meant to be.

There are two distinct countries in Panama, the Pacific Spanish side (Panama City) and the Caribbean Black side, Colon. It is a mix of racism, false pride, economics, and fear that perpetuates the separation, not different than my own fear, or that of many countries. What is bluntly obvious in Panama is the same as in the USA only things are more subliminal in the USA. We are tidy about our race relationships. We pretend better because we know how to make things look good on the surface. I know Colon was not safe for us outside the protection of Duke, which saddened me.

Within two hours we were back at the Panama bus depot negotiating the price for our ride home. The taxis here all have different prices. It is necessary to ask before you enter. I asked the driver why the price was different that when we came. He explained it was night and there were two of us needing a ride. I get the feeling that this is based on the whim of the driver. We asked several taxis' until the price was good. Many drivers are trying to milk the situation and get what they can. The cars have no meters so it is a very strange business, regulated only by the drivers' honesty, which leads to much dishonesty.

When we returned to the apartment, Mario's daughter greeted us. She is a graphic arts teacher at the local university. She was once a contestant for Miss Panama. She was a beautiful woman in her early fifties. We think she and her daughter live somewhere in the large house. She had looked at my watercolor paintings of Colombia and Ecuador. I left them out for Mario, who also paints. It was eight at night. Diana watched her favorite novella and soon we were sleeping and dreaming about the beach we had visited that day.

Day Seven: This morning I was up early, on the balcony, listening to the last bit of music the tropical birds had to offer. Life is pretty darn good. Today we will walk and wander aimlessly until we find something interesting and purposeful. We started the day with a nice breakfast of cereal here in the room. Before we left we asked Mario and Cecelia where an art museum was. They told us about an exhibition at the bank a few blocks away. I showed them photographs on the computer of Ireland and our travels this summer. It was like being home with Diana's parents.

I planned this whole summers traveling itinerary last February. I book the flights six months, or more, in advance to save money. The "side trips" to Panama and Ecuador were placed into the schedule with a little selfishness on my part. We could only stay in Costa Rica for thirty days because of Diana's visa restrictions, which left one month to be in Colombia. That was too long for me to stay at her parents' house. The time there is really so Diana can be with her family, but for me it is not always like I am on a vacation. No matter how nice her parents are. I feel confined in their house. Therefore, the trip to Ecuador, the subsequent return to her parent's home, and the trip to Panama gave us some private time and family time. This last week in Panama is for us to reorganize and spend some quality, alone time. In addition, it is a country where Diana can speak Spanish before she goes back "into the fire" of learning English. I have experienced some of the same hardships she has by traveling in Spanish speaking countries. Not that language is the sole hardship, but I have had a taste of what she has lived through the last year. To not speak the language where you live is not fun. It is like being back in school, learning and asking many questions. Panama is a good steeping stone back to where we are going. It is modern enough to be very comfortable, Spanish speaking, and just rustic enough to make one home sick for nicely paved streets and sidewalks. However, most importantly, a break from the family before we step back into the daily humdrum of New York.

This time together has brought us closer together. I know the whole summer has been a good opportunity for us to get to know each other. I do not feel as temperamental, but I do have my moments of anger. Yesterday I gave Diana a bad time for a few minutes too long. "You never listen to what I say" she shot at me. Boom. My ego gets hurt, and the following conversation spirals into stupidity on my part. She is good for me in that she does not argue back. We managed to get through it, more a credit to her good behavior than mine. She is a better person than me. After translating her English all day I get tired of interpreting. Many things could be taken as criticisms or out of context to what she really means when she uses her English. Diana often says, "Oh, you have a reason". This, at first, was like a waving red flag to a bull. It took me a few weeks to take what she was saying literally, and not get defensive. I have become more patient, but I am far from being all the way there.

After a second effort we went to the bank art exhibition. We did not like the art. It was too busy and a bit disturbing. Rouault, the French artist, did art like this in the last century when he used his black line to outline his subjects. The use of paint was very frenetic and troubling. I am sure some one would say my art is too calm and too lifeless. Such is taste and style.

We returned to the Internet café and Diana called her father. I went online to see how the bank account was looking. Not bad. We had a safety net of two thousand, which we have not touched. I think we did the whole summer on around six thousand. I will know when I return and see the whole bank statement. The money left over will go into the new room we are building in our apartment. It will be spent very soon. I will order the wood and dry wall and we will be ready to begin. Much of the buying this summer has been to decorate the new room.

After the call to Colombia we walked through downtown Panama and headed toward the water where I read about a monument to Balboa. While in route we bought an icy. Then we walked across the wide road that separated the beach from the city. We ate some sandwiches Diana had made of tuna and mixed vegetables. She comes up with some creative dishes that I find strange. However, my attitude about food is to eat what is there and not waste it. My baseline is the poverty in the world. When food is in front of me, I feel lucky to have it. The bay was pretty as we sat there and a nice breeze cooled us, despite the heat being in the upper eighties. The water of the ocean was a muddy dark soup. It smelled and we could see several drainage pipes emptying into the ocean. The trash along the shore and in the water was filthy and it abuses of "our mother". The large boats on the horizon waiting to enter the Panama Canal looked dirty and added to the feeling that it was time to stop such a sad predicament concerning the way the world is polluting our most precious resource, the water.

At the monument I started up a conversation with a young man. I asked him if Balboa was a good or bad man. He said he did not know. I said the conquistadors were not good for the environment or the indigenous peoples. He took our picture and Diana and he began a long conversation. The man had a wife who was pregnant for four months. She had been artificially inseminated because he had an injury while at the police academy which lowered his sperm count. He received a small pension because of his injury. He had traveled to many Central and South American countries. He told Diana that the people on the islands of Colombia had treated him the best. He worked there and said the life was heavenly. He had lived in Costa Rica (Puntarenas) for a while as well. His name was Victor. We said our goodbyes and he jogged back along the costal road. We went across the street and hailed a cab. Many stopped with two men, but we waved them on until one driver stopped with a woman in the front seat. That was acceptable. She wore a nurse uniform and had a stethoscope around her neck that made circumstances even more acceptable.

Our next stop was a return to the shopping mall across from the National Bus Terminal. Diana loves these places. I was raised in the sixties and seventies in a time such places were considered the devil's work. This mall is the largest in Panama and no different than any mall in the world. It was two levels high and had all the brand name stores. Only in the one shop, that sold Panamanian handcrafts and tourists items, did the goods have a local flavor. The factory goods are cranked out and shipped all over the world to such malls. Finding what people make by hand is nearly impossible here. We spent the next two hours walking and then ended by going to a Robin Williams movie about marriage. Ah, it was in English. We enjoyed the break from walking.

Following the movie we caught a cab to the costal shore road that runs along the Panama Canal. It was near sunset. We ate a terrible snack of empanadas (a rolled flat bread with chicken), but the natural juice was great. Soon we walked along the shore to sit and watch a weak sunset. It was because of the clouds. On one side of the road was the canal and the sunset; the opposite side was a bay and the distant city with it's lights and tall buildings. It was romantic and a perfect way to spend the last night of our summer vacation. Tomorrow it's airports and lines of people all stressed. We sat and talked. The lingering "argument" faded as Diana smiled at my jokes and we spoke a little love pact to each other. Our taxi driver, the same man that brought us, returned as we had asked. The ride home cost five dollars.

The driver, like many we had met, was married to a Colombian, and has three children. This soft-spoken man told us about living in both countries, preferring his homeland of Panama. The conversation was in my bad Spanish and Diana's charming Spanish. He had lived in Bogotá for many years and was working as a security guard. He said life was easier in Panama, and that it was very expensive and cold in Bogotá. We had a candid conversation about polities; Chavez in Venezuela, the ridiculousness of the war in Iraq, and hope for a peaceful future. He dropped us at the apartment where we came upstairs, turned on the TV, and I packed the bags. Diana has been watching a soap opera every night. I cannot stomach the predictability of these programs. The novella scenes take all night and it is obvious that the bad guy will not get the girl. It began to rain as the whirling fan set the mood for sleeping.

Day Eight: Yesterday was supposed to be our very last day in Panama. We had packed the luggage the night before, did some touring during the day, and came back to the apartment by two. At four thirty the van came and took us to the airport. At the ticket counter the woman said, "No, you will have a plane tomorrow". It was not clear what she meant exactly. We said we had reservations and that we should not have to wait a day. No, you would have to wait until tomorrow. I was busy weighing the bags and Diana was doing the talking. We were on time, the airline was fully correct, but we had arrived at the airport a full twenty-four hours early. It was not Friday, as I thought, but it was Thursday! Well, better early than late. We apologized to the woman behind the counter, dragged our bags back to the curb with the help of a man who seemed to be with the airlines. He had helped me weigh all the bags and distribute the correct weight from one bag to another. I finally asked him if he worked for the airlines. I had already paid another man with a uniform to take the bags on a cart, and this new man popped out of nowhere. He helped me move the bags and found a taxi, which was a taxi/truck, to take us back to the apartment. After loading all the bags into the open back of the truck I handed him three dollars for three bags. He seemed pissed, but I was not in a mood to feel any compassion. If someone helps me I give a dollar a bag. He thought he deserved more. For me, the extra money and being hassled by this man was more disappointing than the mistake of showing up a day early. I did not ask for help, I had just paid the "real" help, and now he was giving me an attitude.

The truck/taxi was half what we had just paid the van driver whom we reserved a week earlier. (Jose of Panama Taxi, he was the same man that picked us up when we arrived in Panama.) The truck driver was a crazy man. He drove through every parking lot, side street, and even went past all the lines of cars, up the wrong side of the street, to get to where we were going. He blasted the music in his car, because Diana said it was her favorite singer from Mexico. Some of his moves saved time, but many of them made the drive longer because he got stuck in parking lots instead of using the street. He also charged us a dollar to use his cell phone. I forgot to add that when I paid him the fifteen dollars at the end of the drive. The traffic was much worse at that time of day.

We had called Mario on the cell phone from the taxi, and he was home when we arrived back at the place. I gave the doorman some money for helping us and we were back in our room within two hours, but two hours and fifty-two dollars less. Oh well. We called Jose again and explained the mistake. We decided to use the first taxi service, even though he is twice as expensive. Jose, Mario, and Cecelia all asked me if I was leaving on the correct day. I must be bull headed at times not really thinking their humor that funny, but they were right.

Dinner at a Chinese restaurant on the corner was tasty. Diana called her mother whom started off by asking how she was calling from the flying airplane. We went to a small grocery store, bought breakfast, and some additional food. We used half of the Chinese food and the remainder of the food for lunch the following day.

Day Nine: The day itself was very low key, walking miles in the morning, and taxis' in the afternoon. This time we started the day exploring the city by foot. The heat was terrible and it was only 9:00 A.M. Off in the distance, like a beacon of hope, we saw a big shopping mall. This was the most expensive mall in town. The other two we have visited were not exclusive. It was early and nothing was open, so we sat and cooled ourselves off in the air conditioning. We waited for a smoothie drink and had a long conversation with a security guard. He told us where to go and what to see on our last day.

The place we soon headed for was a part of the city I had seen on the bus a few nights before when returning from Colon. It was no mall, but the real shopping street. It was blocks and blocks of open stores with little stalls selling goods on the outer sidewalk. Here and there was a shoe repair booth and lots of people selling lottery chances. I loved it. I told Diana that this was a million times more interesting than a shopping mall. Nothing was predictable, every stall and store was a barrage of stimulation to my senses. I was in my element. Diana put up with it. It was dirty, and a little dangerous; the people were poor, hungry, and looking at us like we were waving money. I found the vegetable street very interesting. The largest papaya I had ever seen sat on open wooden planks with mold growing on the ripe, open sores of the fruit.

Nothing was refrigerated, nothing looked clean, but at the same time it was healthy and natural. The herbs and spices all lay out in the open air and gave off the fragrance of health. This is the real world. This is how the rest of the world lives, survives every day, and does not have a million regulations on how to prepare food. I would like an honest comparison on disease and death between the two worlds. In the developed world we kill our people in hospitals with infections and on the food with pesticides, but how much danger is really lurking in these markets. How many "recalls" of tainted meats come from the processing plants verses the old markets of the world?

We walked out of the open market streets, walked a few blocks to the road that runs along the shore, and found ourselves back at Balboa's monument. We walked a bit further to the park we had eaten lunch the day before and sat on some rocks on a small raised embankment above the shore. We made lunch with some bread we had bought in the market, added cheese, and chicken hot dogs. No one bothered us as we sat in the shade and looked at the dirty bay water. I gave a skinny man what we had not eaten and we moved to a wall that ran along the shore under a huge tree. For an hour we sat and talked as Diana stroked my hair. I lay on the small wall length-wise as three young boys played Tarzan and swung from the long vines that hung from the same tree. A couple of other men lay sleeping on the same wall a few feet away. Other than knowing how dirty the bay water was, we were in heaven. Shortly we would be on an airplane.

Day Ten: So today is our real last day in Panama. Our bags are at the limit. What ever we bought today has to be carried along with the nativity scene we already have in the carry-on handbag. It will be a better last day than the "last day" yesterday. Which was very special.

It is our last few hours until we leave Panama. I am writing on the computer in the airport. We have passed through airport security and the test of our baggage weight. We were two kilos over the mark, but the woman let it slide. I did rearrange two bags, shifting things around. The worst weight offender was a book of

Diana's, which weighed over three kilos. I shifted some cloths between bags. I like Copa Airways for more reason than letting the weight of our bags slide. They are professional and good to people.

In the morning we went to an Internet café to get the phone number of the taxi in New York. The woman who worked there told us about her home island. We had met her the night before in the same Internet business. Her English was so good I asked her where she was from. "The island of Roatan." I had never heard of it before. It is just north of Honduras. She showed us pictures on the Internet and told us in a year she hopes to return home and start a business. It looked heavenly. She said the world's second largest coral reef is there. This is how I gather information for future travel. Little bits and pieces are kept in my memory, and then I add up the coincidences and play a type of roulette that is based on first hand references from strangers.

We walked out of the store and caught a taxi for the Museum of Contemporary Art. The second we entered the door we recognized the photographs from the same exhibition we had seen in Bogotá of world news photography. I still wanted to see it again. This time we had to pay, but who cares. The compelling photos made me sick because of the graphic depiction of war. How can humans be so cruel? One would think photography would raise people's awareness of how bad we are as a species. Does art change the world?

We began to walk along a narrow busy street with no sidewalk, so I asked Diana to cross onto a safer side. As we walked we saw a store I had seen several times from inside our taxis on this route. The store was called "Linen House". We went inside and one hundred and eighty dollars later, exited. We found tablecloths and linens that were way out of our price range in the USA. We bought a banquet tablecloth that was forty dollars. I am sure it would be over three hundred dollars in the States. They also had Mallas (the Panamanian fabric made by the Indians). All the prices were better than we had seen on the streets sold by the Indians. We bought more hand-sown tablecloths and table linens that were beautiful. It was a chance to buy things we will have all of our lives. The only problem is, we do not have a big dinning room table, and we do not even have a kitchen table in our tiny apartment. However, some day, who knows how good we will have it. The plan is to put Diana through school, again, so she makes a profession in the States. The last day cost us an extra two hundred dollars, but we found a gold mine. The man who sold us the product was from Indian. He spoke perfect English and Spanish. We even bought Diana some hand-embroidered blouses. They were twenty dollars each. We bought several gifts for friends for Christmas.

The salesman in the store told us not to go to the area known as Santa Ana. Somehow the topic of where we were going next came up. We were heading to the old city. He said it was not safe at the cathedral that was to be our next destination. He hailed a taxi we took to the causeway that runs along the canal. We had been there two nights before. This time we went into the shops, after we sat on the waters edge and ate what was left overs from the Chinese restaurant. We sat in the hot sun and ate looking at the ships. After lunch we walked along the water and found a beautiful apricot tree. The breeze was delicious and the temperature perfect in the shade. I could see someone had sat there before eating freshly picked apricots, leaving many seeds on the ground. The big boats were going and coming into the canal. Sitting watching boats takes me back in time. For many centuries humans traveled by boat to far off lands, the nostalgia of those times permeates at the Panama Canal.

We still were hungry so we went to a restaurant and ordered rice and fried yucca. In a short time and we were in a cab back to the apartment. When we got in Mario told us that the taxi driver, Jose, had called and moved our pickup time forward an hour. It was fine with me; we were an hour ahead of schedule anyway. In half an hour we showered and were ready to leave. We said our second goodbyes and arrived at the airport four hours before our departure.

I was talking to Diana about how important it has been for us to get away and spend this time together. It has been a test of our marriage. To travel is a true test of ones character, and a double test of a relationship. I think traveling both challenges and glues love together. Traveling is a very stressful thing to do. It is full is uncertainty and at times, out and out fear. One's radar has to be on constantly. Looking people in the eye is half the ticket to staying safe. Reading taxi driver's character in a tiny, rear view mirror, or by the sound of their voice, is crucial. Knowing when to cross the street and leap into traffic together creates a rhyme of togetherness. I think most people are instinctive travelers.

One of my uncomfortable moments with Diana is when she is afraid, or has fear when nothing bad is happening. One day she went up to the police and asked them if it was dangerous where we were. "If you look for trouble, trouble will find you", the policeman wisely answered. The same goes with fear. I have been robbed once and that was enough to teach me a life lesson. I left my bag a few feet away and was distracted by a team of thieves, one talked while the other walked with my valuables in a small bag. The taxi driver who gave us a ride home from the airport last night was a man of poor character. We decided to spend the extra fifteen dollars and go with a person we knew. A man who drives like a maniac and honks his horn at woman on the street is not a person to trust a second time. We have to size up people and continuously make judgments as to any future business. It's luck, karma, and knowledge that leads us through life.

I cannot think of a more pleasant person to be with than Diana. It has been a year and we are more and more a couple every day. I feel very honored and lucky to have found such a gift. The gamble and risks have been worth the effort. Next year we hope to go to Europe. Diana has always dreamed of Italy and Greece. We will save our money and buy the tickets in December. As I am sitting here writing on the computer Diana is rubbing my bare foot. How lucky can a man be? How strange is life? A couple of years ago I was tortured by the end of a long relationship. This is only the beginning of our love. How much better will this be? I am sure beyond my best dreams. We leave for home in an hour.

Chapter 15. Costa Rica Christmas

We have been here in Costa Rica for two days now. This is the second morning. Our luggage was lost. My biggest concern is the motorcycle gear I bought for my friend Jose. It was in the luggage. Our clothes are already here in the apartment because we keep them stored here. I had the iPod charger and speakers in the luggage, but most of the other items were not important.

When we arrived Jose was at the airport. On the ride home, we stopped at a restaurant with the young girl that baby-sits his son. As we sat there Jose and I began to discuss instant karma. We were discussing all the important spiritual aspects of life. I am reading a book about religion and how it is destroying the world. We discuss everything like two best friends. All these years we have created a bond that I need with another man. Sometimes I just need to call him, and talk from the States. I am at peace after being able to tell him my hassles with my job, or whatever ails me. Here in Costa Rica I have this friend that recharges me because we share many of the same philosophies about change. The focus has to be within ones self. He reminds me of this.

Tonight the three of us sat on a log on the beach and watched the sunset. Usually Jose has his son with him, but his baby Kailani is in California with his mother. I was watching Jose's face and how happy he was to just sit and watch the sunset. At the same time I see how Diana and he are becoming friends. How can anyone not like Diana? She is so full of joy and life. There must be a million times a day I note, silently to myself, how she has many good qualities. I tell her too, but the inner reflection is so important in building and maintaining love. Diana points out to me how nasty I have been at times in the last year. I can only explain my actions as fear based and that the relationship was so new. We did not really know each other when we got married. I do not feel as cranky toward her. I am much more patient.

Today I got on her about cooking me too much food again. I would rather feel like I am in control of my own diet. When she makes me food it is twice as much as I need. I have had to work so hard at keeping my weight down. I know how easy it is to binge on food. I see Diana bingeing and I get at her about it. Bingeing is not just the mouth full of food. It is the secret eating that we all do behind the backs of others. I pick at food too. I know how important it is to keep food away from being in reach. The basic concept is to feel like I have full awareness of my consumption. We all battle at giving in to weaknesses that slowly kill us. Diana knows I am honest with her about this in her and myself.

We have had many conversations about getting married so quickly. Diana gives me three reasons why she married me. One; She was too old in her country. She was an old maid already. "In my country if you don't marry by 28, no one will want you." Two: She fell in love with my words in the emails. Even though I used a translation program that mixed up most of the words, my real personality came through. On the surface I was too old for her, but the real me was shining through. I think the our inner being is what is most important. Our surface traits are just that. The looks, the economic status, and employment status are not what real "character" is. I am lucky that my soul was read in those emails as well. Third: The job Diana had already applied for in New York. She had her momentum already set in the direction of New York. I suppose it was like the momentum I had set by having a young female friend with a child here in Costa Rica, before I met Diana. I was friends with a woman years younger than me. I was learning Spanish. I was bonding with people (only the true bond comes in marriage, not in friendship). All I know is that Diana and I clicked, and we are still clicking. Tonight she told me that we are so busy and occupied in New York that our time on this trip to Costa Rica is just for the two of us; together. A woman that knows how to keep love alive is everything to me.

Diana prays a lot. At first I thought I married a nut job because she was always muttering, even when she wakes in the morning. In the car the first thing she does is start muttering. I finally asked her once. What are you saying? I thought she was talking to herself about her problems. Maybe that is what praying is anyway, but it gives me a certain peace to know she has a spiritual vocabulary always going. As much as I hate religion, I see how necessary it is to have a dialogue with God, or whatever one chooses to call the energy that brought us where we are.

The Catholic religion really makes me angry, but I am very tolerant with her about it. I see nothing good that would come by pointing out the hypocrisy to her. I talk about it, but not as a personal attack. I know the bottom line is respecting her practices even if I can only share a small bit. My faith is "eclectic" compared to Diana's, which is a little naive. That may seem like an arrogant statement, but I have studied other perspectives of belief and see so many parallels, not a single answer. Maybe what is "naive" is a more pure state of worship, I do not know. I see a complex answer; Diana has a very simplistic approach.

I am positive that Diana believes that Mary was a virgin and Christ is the Son of God. I wonder deeply if it makes any difference to the quality of a person's life if they believe that Mary was a virgin. Does believing in the Virgin birth make a person a better Christian? How can this belief make me a better person? In addition, how dare any religion tell me they know I am saved, or damned, based on a doctrine? The works of my life, how I treat others, and what influences I have on others is between the maker and myself, no one else. I see all teachings as a way to make myself a better, more aware person. My trinity is Krishna, Buddha, and Christ. When I tell Diana that I believe all the Gods are the same God she cringes. My cynicism about Catholicism has lead me to believe in a different manor. My premise is that I hold the question dearer than the answer. In addition, most importantly, if there is a God, that God wants me to question everything, even if She (as in Woman) has existence.

I am fed up with the pretense of "high quality" as being something better. Better than what? The spectrum of this state of "bulls--t" goes from religion, to economics, and to standards of living. Who says that a meal cooked on a beach by a local woman in her kitchen is of a poorer quality than of a chef in a fine French restaurant. The nature of real quality is a myth to me. I see this hype in art, on TV, in religion, music, and literature; you name it.

Fine art is propaganda for the rich to show off their wealth. It is prostitution on a refined scale with a brand name. I am fed up with the hype that comes with the best-flavored toothpaste, and the best restaurants, to the best governments (that kill in the name of democracy). Most ideas and products have been polluted with a pretense of "refinement". Why is a clean floor in a cheap restaurant any worse than a clean tiled floor with the finest Italian marble? Food turns into poop no matter how expensive it was. Get over it!

I found my wife in a far off place. I was looking for a situation with as little hype as possible. My set of expectations fit hers, but it had nothing to do with trying to meet some high standard, high society, or criteria of "class". There is a state of being in living ones life that has nothing to do with pretense, or evaluated status. In fact, most people in the world live this way. The problem I see is that the newer generations do not know the difference between natural survival and life with unnecessary expectations. The mold has been cast by television and movies, which are entertainment and not reality. Realistic expectations are what life should be based on, such as truth in a simple marriage ceremony.

Maybe I am not writing my words clear enough because hypocrisy is in everything we do and say, but there is an important simple truth that needs to be found in our lives. An expensive wedding is a good example of how couples start off on the wrong foot. By wanting the "best" young people strive for the pretense of having wealth. For a day the big limo and the expensive party is a fantasy of how wealthy people live. The pressure to put on this air of luxury is overwhelming and a very sad affair. Who can keep up with that level of pretense? This false ideal begins with the marriage ceremony and soon transmits into a purchase of a new home, and on and on and on. It is impossible to have everything one needs. However, who in American society is saying there are real limits to what one can have in life? From the TV commercials to the government's propaganda there are no limits to our freedoms and our economic aspirations. The sky is the limit as we plunder into debt. The sky is the limit as we rape the environment. The trap of modern America is that money is a false illusion. Young couples start with expensive ceremonies, spends it like they have it, when they do not. We use natural resources like we own them, we do not. I am proud to say my wedding ceremony cost one thousand dollars. I am not proud of any judgments that will come with people knowing this, but I am free and clear of any debt. The same applies to our honeymoon. We did not spend what we did not have. I had to learn some of these lessons the hard way.

I remember I went to a hotel near my house in New York. The honeymoon suite was three hundred and fifty dollars for the night. I talked about this with Diana and she refused to spend the money. I was being pressured by a friend to "go for it and give her a night she would always remember". Well, we stayed home; spread rose petals all over the bed and burned candles. The union was real. The hype was left out of the room. I may seem like I'm boasting, but the real recognition is that the "battle" of keeping things real and simple often conflicts with the pretense of what is customary and expected. It is like people who buy art because they know it will have a financial value verses something that appeals to their sense of beauty. Some people cannot see or feel beauty without feeling the extra layer of pretense. Money corrupts when simple, straightforward pleasure is the real object of value.

When I was young I would make my mother a Mothers Day card. My father called me cheap because I would not spend my money on a Hallmark card. I wanted to make a personal statement to show my mother that the time I spent creating was a labor of love. My father never understood my aesthetic goals, and to this day maybe the arguments I have with his values are reverberated in my approach to life. That conflict had given me a premise that to this day is my credo. I feel liberated by my freedom to reject, to deny, and rebel against a culture that is steeped in false illusions. Even though Diana and I are twenty years apart, her roots in Colombia are those of an equal value. How lucky can one man be? I attribute most of her awareness to her spiritual practice and her awareness to the real value of love and generosity. I have done enough to keep my life in sync. Diana inspires me to be more.

This is our fourth day here. I woke in a bad mood, and then I turned on the TV to see that Bhutto was killed in Pakistan. I lived in Pakistan and was there when her father was President. He was later killed. Hung by the military. A suicide bomber has killed her. What a perverse world, where killing is insane. I have a strong affinity for the Pakistani people because of the time and age when I lived there. Hatred for the West was not like now and I saw a country that was full of promise and becoming modern. I went about freely and was never in any fear. I had so much trouble with my father that my adventures there were a good way to keep distracted from my family. A war broke out and we were evacuated to Tehran, Iran for several months. So I feel sensitive to a country that brings me fond memories from that important time in my life.

My mood was made worse by some miscommunications between Diana and I. Sometimes she does not understand my English and misses my point. Sometimes I am just in a bad place. Yesterday was a waste because we spent the entire day going to get the luggage. The luggage was in the airport, but it took much time to retrieve and we had to wait three hours until the next bus to return to Jaco. We went to a Chinese restaurant and then went to the church to sit for a while. Diana went and bought some antibiotics because she has a sinus infection. She still has this today, which adds to the lack of good mood in the day.

The "miscommunication" was about changing the house, or having Diana rearrange some of the things here. She started by wanting to move a lamp cover. It is hanging over the dining room table. I went to great effort to put it up, and the very room she wanted to move it into is where it hung for almost a year before. One of the biggest issues in the marriage have been my stuff verses her taste. She came with two suitcases and everything else in the house was mine. However, she managed to take half of my things down because she saw my house as too busy and cluttered. It is admittedly full of things, but I needed to be communicated with, first, concerning the changes. The day she did this move was the day I was busy working on the new room. I felt that she did this behind my back while I was literally not looking. Therefore, she started in about moving this here, taking that down, and I went mad for a few minutes. She is not taking my wishes into consideration. She wants what she wants. Then accuses me of dominating the house decorations. Her reaction is worse. "When I get my house and car, I will do it the way I want".

I opened my entire life and house to her and she feels controlled. It is a difficult psychological area to maneuver through. It is not the end of this struggle, but today I put my foot down. In anger I told her to leave things the way they are. To me I would never go into her room in Colombia and start to change things around. I see it that simply. Yes, she needs to nest and make a home. I really need to be talked to and feel like my wishes are respected. She tells me that in Colombia the woman decides everything about the house. I think a man can cook, clean, and decorate just as competently as a woman.

We have seen, or been visited by, many people today. Jose came in the morning, and then we saw a woman and her child who lives here in the complex. Then, Oscar, the man I bought the house from came while Diana was at the beach. Oscar will return later this afternoon also. Another man named Al walked by and came into the house. He is around 62 years old, a retiree with a child that is nine months old. He and I met about three years ago. He is from California and worked for the Chamber of Commerce. Al has written a mystery novel and sold enough to break even after self-publishing. He has had two children with his Costa Rican wife, and has a house in San Jose as well as the condo here in Jaco. The first day we met we talked in the Jacuzzi for about an hour. We hit it off right away. The condo's here have a whole list of characters that I have met over the years. They are my neighbors. Many people come and go, but the owners and a few renters are consistently present. Many of the Americans here are from the seedy side of life. They rent long enough to get behind on the rent and have to leave. There are many "druggies" here too, people who come here for the cheap and easy access to drugs.

The drug underground is present in the lifestyles of many young Americans who come here and stay. The jobs pay nearly nothing, but the rent and drugs are cheap. It is a problem in that the "real working" Americans are not represented. The hard working, tax paying, family oriented people are too busy working to find time to fall through the cracks and get on the crack. The older I get the more I have seen the misuse of drugs as a real problem. In middle class America drugs are a right of passage for the young into adulthood. However, in the ghettos it is a matter of life and death. If a person does drugs next to me I do not care. I have seen them shoot up in Amsterdam, and smoke weed on the beaches here in Jaco. I would not call the police because some people use recreationally, while other heavy users are out to hurt themselves and others. However, the situation is too ambiguous for me to call the law when the police are as big a part of the problem as the addicts. I say build rehab houses, not jails. I know in the future this social problem will be handled in a way that is much more humane. I am lucky to have never been arrested for smoking pot when I did, but I really do not see the harm in it if no one is harming himself or herself. The same goes with alcohol and cigarettes. Jaco is not a drug haven any more than any place, this country or the States. It is here because the underground drug culture is everywhere in the world. When governments stop repressing this behavior and taxing the use of such substances, then the world will begin to be a safer place. (As ironic as this may sound to some people, it is true!)

Today was Friday. It is December 28. I had a small tiff with Jose about not paying me the money for the motorcycle gear. Two days went by and I finally asked him for the money. His response was that he was not a mind reader and that I needed to tell him. However, really, he should have never taken the motorcycle gear without giving me the money immediately. Asking, "Do you want your money?" is just a bulls--t ploy. I was pretty good about the whole thing and was doing well until I said he was not living in full integrity. These attacks never work well. He was using the "cultural difference" excuse also. "You are family, that's why I thought it was ok". Me, "It was ok when I said so last night. But I ran low on money today and it wasn't ok by the time you left in the morning without paying". In my book if you do a person a favor they ask of you, you do not put them off. You do not leave the responsibility up to them to ask to be paid when you bought something they asked you to.

I was imagining that he did not have the money, and I was even going to ask for the things back until he paid up. He also kept us waiting for many hours we had suggested a trip to another beach by car. Maybe I am compulsive, but if I say something to someone or make a proposed venture, or if I cannot do it, I acknowledge my original offer and explain myself. Last summer when we were here in Costa Rica there were many days when Jose kept me waiting and showed up hours late, or even cancelled things we had planned. Yes, sure the Tico (A word for Costa Rican) way is not the American way, and things are very laid back here. However, I get fed up with the "this is my culture" and we are different than you. A word is a word, and keeping your word is important in any country. If I did not keep my word and did not bring him the motorcycle clothes he wanted, he would have been just as disappointed in me. It all passed. I know I was in a correct place and he did pay me. However, being asked, "Do you want your money" several times is nonsense. Its like saying, "Would you like me to pay you the money I said I would pay you?" "Duh!" Therefore, I called him on it. This is what friends need to do sometimes. Lovers, friends and spouses all have to work at not being lazy and keeping in full integrity. It was a twenty-minute ride to the beach we were going to, but soon the small talk filled in the tension and the laughter came fourth. We were telling each other how important our friendship is in a matter of minutes.

I know my anger gets the best of me. Even if I do not express the full Monty of rage, the smallest amount poisons my mood. I was telling this small personal attribute to Diana and she was kind enough to agree with me, and continued to point out a few more flaws in my character. How kind of her. I can take criticism, but I just do not like to. When we were exchanging differences, Jose kept telling me that it was "your (my) reality", and not his to be so punctual about the transactions. I have bought things in the States before for him and we did not go through this. I also explained how insecure I get when money runs low like it did today. I had made enough purchases today to be down to my last twenty dollars. One of the buys was a necklace for my sarcastic wife. The other was some roofing cement. Waiting for people, standing in lines, and being talked about are my favorite things.........not!

At one point today Diana was visiting with Eric, the head security guard here in the condos. She kept saying something to me in Spanish that I did not understand. She said it three times and I finally got pissed, "Say it in English". I took it as a rude gesture to cut me out, and put me in a position where I was being talked down to because of the language barrier. I called her on that as we rode our bicycles to the beach. When we come to Costa Rica or Colombia she speaks mostly Spanish to me. (I am sure it is some kind of reaction to English being the dominant language at home.) When she is speaking Spanish I am genuinely happy for her. In fact, I made myself busy so she could have some alone time with Eric. I know she needs to have friends and I know she needs to speak her own language. She bubbles over when she can speak her own language. The shoe is on the other foot when I am here in a Spanish speaking country. I want to learn Spanish, so I can better communicate with my wife, and the only chance I really get is when I am forced into this situation in Costa Rica or Colombia. When I speak I am better at projecting what I want rather than understanding what is being said to me.

I rode the bicycle to the hardware store yesterday. I knew the Spanish word for resin, but not for the chemical that cleans out the sewer pipes. I got my point across, using "caca" and holding my nose. I also got a few laughs for my crude immature use of their language, but it worked. I like the challenge of having to communicate when I am learning Spanish. At what point does a person speak a language? Is it a few baby steps, or is it only when I can fluently read a newspaper. I say the first few words make the classification of "speaker" a justification. "Do you speak Spanish?" "No but if you hum a few words in place of words you don't know, it really works". Much of understanding a language, even if you do not speak it, is body language, and the knowledge of how typical conversations are structured.

There are times I listen to Diana and know I am the only person on earth that is speaking her strange language. I know all her mispronounced words. Some times I have to just come out and tell her she is not speaking English. I am not going to lie and say it is easy. To speak a different language than your wife is something I never thought in a million years would be a problem. There are times when we just do not have a clue what the other person is saying. Of course, I suppose it is my creative abilities that get me through. It may be partially true, but the attraction to each other is the real key to this relationship. We are a very unlikely match that must give many people much to gossip about, but really there has to be more than attraction and fun. It is a mutual need and a sense that we are going somewhere together in life, and getting things done.

As close as it came to not happening last year, this marriage in itself has been one great accomplishment after another. We talk about the future and how we want certain things. She wants to help her parents and have children. I can agree with half of the statement. Diana goes though moods about wanting children, other times she accepts my resistance. I notice the talk about children always comes into conversation around the time she is about to ovulate. This biology I cannot control. She will ask me about names for a boy. The girls name is already Isabella. The name I approve of, but the expected expense can make my hippie freedom vanish into dirty diapers and sleepless nights. Am I lazy for not wanting a child at age 56? Am I selfish when the world is so over populated? We have China going on in every corner of every country? I also have this Hindu belief that if you bear a child you are bound to the wheel of life at least one more time before the ultimate liberation of your soul. (See how nicely I have twisted a religious belief to fit my own selfish goals. I do not eat meat, but I wear leather.) I do not think Diana has a clue to how drastic her life would change if she were a mother. It is like watching a young girl playing dolls. Only this doll is expensive, and a full life commitment, and a ton of potential trouble in the teen years. Am I afraid or enlightened?

Yes the biological time bomb is ticking, but I think she needs to anchor herself first. Why have a baby at sea when an island of economic security and professional stability could be a port of prosperity. I do not think it wise to long for what you do not have. Although, I longed for the kind of wife I have and Diana fits many, if not all, the needs a man longs for. I can see how attractive she is through others, yet the down side is her innocence and lack of worldly experiences, which cause me to feel more like a parent than a lover. She is not built in the same mold I came from. I need to remember this always. The blissful angel and the difficult demon come knocking at the door. The demon is hard work and responsibilities. Life is not always a Costa Rican vacation.

We spent a great deal of the day doing laundry. Because of the tropical humidity, all of the sheets and clothes get a mildew odor that is bad. Our washing machine broke, so we went to Jose's place to use his washer. I did it because Diana was too shy to go to Jose's house without being formally invited. He was at work, so I went at it like a mad man. We needed a dryer more than anything, but did not have one. Our apartment was a sea of sheets and clothes on every imaginable surface. We had all the fans running. We will dry them, put them in plastic bags and hope the next time we return that the house does not smell like a mold factory. Eric suggested we open the windows a slight amount, which I will do when we leave Sunday night on the 5PM bus.

I love it here. I love being with my wife and good friend Jose. There is really not that much to complain about, but I will find something to gripe about anyway. It is about midnight and I want to stretch out every second of this vacation. I can stay up late when we are here.

One last note before I retire: On this day every year the Costa Rican newspapers write false, funny, and fictitious stories. I heard of this a few years ago. They make fun of the press by printing outlandish news events that did not really happen. The people in turn play tricks on each other. It is a kind of "April's Fool's Day". Jose called a friend today and asked her if she knew who was in the hospital? She got all upset and Jose said he would get back to her. He hung up before he told her who was in the hospital. A few minutes later he called back and said, "hello". The woman, of course is instantly baiting him for an answer. After worrying for many minutes; He replied, "Well, the doctors, the nurses, and the patients are all in the hospital". I got a good laugh about that. Jose came over for dinner and the same woman called him saying she needed to be taken to a clinic because she had a toothache. He went off to help only to discover that he was part of a return prank. This is the kind of people here that keep life fun and lighthearted.

We met an American man while riding the bikes yesterday. His name is Will. I liked his shirt, so I said, "Nice shirt". He said, "Let me ask you something". His son brought the shirt from Bali. He went on to tell me a long story. I could not quite follow because he went into great detail about a rip off and the inflated bill at a local restaurant. On the street I have a few seconds to size someone up. He seemed honest. The conversation changed to him asking me about sights in Costa Rica. He is also a schoolteacher of fourth and fifth grades in a town called Fall Mill River, California. I liked him right away. Diana stood behind us as we spoke for about five minutes.

Later in the night we were walking back from our dose of Thi Che, a drink with cinnamon and cardamom. We have a habit of going to this one shop and ordering this cold drink that is heavenly. Sometimes we have skipped dinner only to be filled by this drink that we both are crazy about. We ran into Will again. His wife is Mary. They were both also out for the night, strolling on the main street. Jaco is so small that it is easy to run into people two or three times in a day. This time Will was wearing a white t-shirt. Mary was walking with him and we started to talk again. Will suggested we go get a fruit drink somewhere, so we went to a local bar and sat in these huge chairs made of solid thick wood. Mary is a retired kindergarten teacher. She is tall, attractive and looks very Irish.

We sat for maybe an hour and talked. Mary and Diana hit it off right away while Will and I continued our dialogue. Will and I have much in common. I told him he is a kindred spirit. We had many common life stories. We invited them over for lunch after we walked to our condo and showed them where we live. At noon the following day they stopped by the house. Will brought his Ukulele and sang a song he wrote. It was a very nice and catchy song. It was a song about his son.

At lunch he was telling me how special fatherhood is. He almost had me convinced. It was very pleasant to meet new people. I hope we can see them again this summer in Europe. They got a free airline ticket to Europe this summer for being bumped off a flight. I was also very happy that Diana made a friend and was able to make a new connection with a woman. It is important for her. Mary was saying to me that if Diana and I had a child, Diana would never leave me. It is a funny way of putting things, but I am more interested in making sure the relationship is solid in other ways. The economics of a partnership are very important to me.

I sang the song I wrote for Diana at our wedding. We told them how she was distracted while I was singing to her at the wedding. Diana did not understand enough English when she first arrived. She told us how the woman that put on her false eyelashes warned her not to cry. So Diana was stone faced while I was pouring my heart out in song. I remember how the minister was looking at Diana in a kind of disbelief. Also, none of us knew that she did not understand what was being sung to her. I do not realize how difficult it has been for her. I have mentioned this paradox before. I thought I was giving out the keys to heaven; instead the dear woman was going through hell. Mary was telling me how difficult the first year of their marriage was. She said if it were not for the legal papers, she might have left. I know at times Diana was equally as frustrated. She put up with outburst from me. In my defense I can only say that it was equally as difficult to go trough as many changes all at once. However, there was really no other way to do it. Kierkegaard's leap of faith was shared by both of us and through it all we did survive.

In a very literal and simplistic view, marriage is lovemaking. It takes time to tell ones partner how to go about what pleases the most and where the touching is most effective. For me there has been an element of healing taking place as well. I felt so violated by the last relationship that even though three years had passed, I was still dealing with residual anger. Maybe that anger goes back as far as childhood. We reinvent and heal ourselves through relationships with others. Maybe the only way to move on in life is to find a new partner and build a life together. I believe we are not whole as people unless we can find meaning through another. Yes, I also believe that a person has to be whole and happy with them-selves, in order to be capable of finding real love. It is really a juggling process where we balance ourselves with the acts of loving others and self-love.

We arrived back in New York today. Life has some miracles that are unexplainable. In the airport I met a Vice-Principal of a school district that is very close in population to my school district. We sat down next to him in the airport and struck up a conversation about living in neighboring towns. It was good to meet a person who is an educator and discuss some of the fun parts, and the distressing parts, of our work. His name was Bob. He pointed out how the schools on Long Island are so segregated because of money. I called it "economic segregation or apartheid American style". Because the schools are based on property taxes, there is a huge injustice in the distribution of equal education. The funding differences that occur from one town to the next are incredible. A rich school district can be a few minutes from the poorest. In America this is our last great shame, a hidden scar. We do not give equal opportunity when the have-nots live in clear view of excessive wealth and have no access to that wealth.

We went to our boarding area and they asked for four volunteers and offered a two hundred dollar voucher. I approached the reception but was there to see if they would increase the value of the voucher. They did not. We soon boarded the airplane and I sat next to a woman who is a photography teacher in a local (rich) district. The conversation was mostly about curriculum, but I spoke about the drastic funding differences as well. We spoke for an hour at least. It was so delightful to find another teacher within a three-day span. This time I found a person discussing counter points to my situation. We had a creative discourse about curriculum and what to teach. This is why I love to travel. Traveling magically puts me in contact with those I need to talk with. The openness that is present is so valuable and energizing.

I could have gone years and never met Will, Bob, and Clare (the photography teachers), yet in a matter of days I am able to link up, and free up some pent-up feelings. Yes, I like letting off some steam with strangers, and it make me feel human again. The situation with my job is a real problem right now. After eight years of taking my students out of doors, the administration has padlocked my door. Under the guise of security for the students they have denied the students the one opportunity to experience nature while being educated. This is a most bazaar but true, event. Not only did the head of security harass me in front of students for having the door unlocked, but the Principal had the door pad locked forever. He knew I had taken them outside for years. I had a meeting with the union representative, but other than an apology from the head of security for his inappropriate yelling, the door remains locked. Therefore, I have had the chance to at least share this with other professionals and let off some steam. I told this appalling story to the other photography teacher. She said, "You have to use sunlight to teach photography". I feel like I work in a prison.

On the train that returned us to our car we spoke with two men from Holland. I crave these spontaneous contacts as brief as they are. The men were speaking in their native tongue. Diana and I were trying to guess their language. Dutch! This opened up a five minutes conversation when I finally asked them if they were speaking Danish, or what. The men are truck drivers and take loads of cargo containers around Holland. One of the guys asked Diana if she was single and she explained I was her husband. This is a common event when people, rather men, see her and try to make a connection. I was speaking with the other man, so the second fellow subtly asked her on the side. I know I am old enough to be her father, but wonder what men are thinking by asking any woman with another man if they can have a date.

There is a taxi driver in Jaco that speaks to Diana while he drives us from the grocery store. He has tried to get her to go out with him. This is a very comical thing to me, but Diana feels insulted by it. It is not that I am laughing at her. I am not her keeper. Most men feel they have to put the relationship in a cage for protection. The Latino men are very possessive. If they are not with a woman they are very flirtatious. That is putting it politely. Many times the conversation is in Spanish so I am not paying full attention to what is being said. I really think desperate men act out of desperation when they are so blatant. They do not know that being polite is more important than getting laid in the eyes of a woman. I also know that jealousy is a poison that kills love. This kind of thing has happened often even in the States. I don't know if I should play the role of the macho protector. Usually I watch these men make fools of themselves, then politely step into the conversation to break it up.

Our eight-day journey ended with a drive home and a warm bath. We needed to relax after the air travel. The TV was soon on and we watched "Shrek". I fell asleep with my head on Diana's lap. Now, a few hours later, I cannot sleep. Diana woke up long enough to wish me a Happy New Year. We said a small prayer and showed our thanks for each other. The fireworks outside marked the opening of what I know will be a wonderful year with a wonderful woman.

New Entry: We are back one week from Costa Rica. It has been a difficult week. My point of reference is one week ago yesterday we lie under a palm tree and fell asleep in the hot wind. I suppose that is a bad reference point because life is not lying around under palm trees all day. This weekend we went to two movies, both had sad and depressing endings. The one about a boy in Afghanistan was "The Kite Runner". We went to see a second movie on the next night so we could sign papers for Diana's life insurance. Our friend met us after the movie, and before for a quick bite of food. His wife is from Afghanistan. We met at my church years ago because, by sheer coincidence, her English teacher in Afghanistan was a girlfriend of mine, years afterwards. Many miles and many years between all three of us created a new friendship. The Afghan woman's husband is whom we bought the insurance policy from.

Diana was telling me, before she got married, her friends warned her not to get life insurance. There was a story that had been circulating in Colombia about an American man who insured his wife then killed her for the money. A series of questions from Diana and explanations on the subject made me upset. Then Diana started talking to the Afghan woman saying, "It is a problem, Dennis doesn't want babies". This made the evening more stressful. Of course I understand needing to know what one signs and every detail that comes with it. Apart from that, the baby issue will only get worse if she wants to make it a big issue. Diana's view is that life insurance is only for people with children.

I did not have any insurance until a few years ago. My policies are very small. The rest of my "money" (ha, ha) is in mutual finds for retirement. Diana said to me this morning that she did not want any money from my death and wanted me to change my beneficiaries on my policies back to my niece. This only made me more angry and upset. When we had the scare about a cyst in Diana's breast I began to worry about death and the realistic thought that I maybe paying for a funeral. The cyst was removed and my fears were silenced, but still, life insurance is weird. There is perversion and comfort in the security that comes with life insurance. Death gets a pay off.

Some of Diana's views are self-centered. Some of them are just plain unsophisticated. However, many of them in her heart are correct because her innocence is pure. How I work through these times and differences is very important. I get angry and that is destructive. I get defensive and that is counter productive. When Diana is weak and crying I want to force instant answers and that does not work. I remain her beneficiary, but she has asked me to assign money to her mother in the event of her dying. I will honor this request.

After the vacation in Costa Rica I have been depressed about my job and that affects my awareness in the marriage. The foolishness of the students and lack of support from my administrators puts me in a funk. I see how much energy the student's waste, how directionless their lives are, and I feel a sense of loss. They fill their lives with entertainment. They distract their five senses, thinking all the while they are achieving "fun". The administrators are so full of themselves that controlling the school is more important than being human and flexible. I cannot get over my door to the outside world being locked. I cannot get over the fact that my students cannot just step out into the sunshine and take a simple photograph. The alternatives given by the administration are to have security lead escorts out the back of the building. This is totally unrealistic. I feel like I am in prison and no matter what I try to do to work my thoughts in a positive direction, it fails. One administrator's inappropriate jokes at the beginning of the year, about my marriage lasting only two years, hasn't helped my attitude either.

Therefore, I have been writing and hope I can write my way out of this funk. I got my first clear overview of this book today. There is a photographic light at the end of the tunnel. I can also now envision what the book will physically look like.

There is no real ending to this book because our lives together will continue and have many more adventures. The conflicts and joys are a part of life's ebb and flow. Our life together is very typical and somewhat mundane. When we leave the country and have summers together, I live in my own movie. It is not a Hollywood movie where there is some invented violence or twisted plot of intrigue, suspense, or betrayal. Like so many people we work hard and have fun playing. Like so many others we have created a union that is simple and wonderful to share. We have bought our tickets for Europe next summer. It will be our last full summer together until Diana finishes her degree. Diana has a job next fall with the company in New York City she applied to three years ago. In the last few weeks Diana passed her drivers license test and I have worked through my depression about my job. Some day I hope Diana will write a counter point to this book and tell her side of this love story. There is no end, in fact today Diana took the car out and drove alone for the first time.